Harry Thompson

Harry Thompson was the inventor of many TV comedy series including *Have I Got News For You* and *Da Ali G Show*. He was the author of several acclaimed bestsellers including *Peter Cook: A Biography* and *Penguins Stopped Play*, as well as a historical novel *This Thing of Darkness*, shortlisted for the Booker Prize. He worked as a producer at Talkback TV and in his spare time ran an infamous cricket team, the Captain Scott XI. Harry Thompson died in 2005.

Praise for *Tintin: Hergé and His Creation*

'A delightful portrait . . . well-organised and well-researched . . . witty, fascinating and just a little mad . . . it is more or less impossible not to like this book' *European*

'An admirably organised double biography . . . For specialists and for the myriad devotees of the stories this book is a must' *Sunday Express*

'As a broad, bright Hergé-like brush-stroke, it has genuine appeal' *Guardian*

'The first book in English on Tintin to have an idea in it' *The Times*

'Immensely detailed . . . it contains a great deal of fascinating information' *GQ*

T0385338

Tintin

Hergé and His Creation

HARRY THOMPSON

JOHN MURRAY

First published in Great Britain in 1991 by Hodder & Stoughton
An Hachette UK Company

This paperback edition first published in Great Britain in 2011 by
John Murray (Publishers)
An Hachette UK Company

5

A CIP catalogue record for this title is available from the British Library

ISBN 978-1-84854-672-1
Ebook ISBN 978-1-84854-673-8

Typeset in Bembo by Servis Filmsetting Ltd, Stockport, Cheshire

Printed and bound by Clays Ltd, St Ives plc

John Murray policy is to use papers that are natural, renewable and recyclable products
and made from wood grown in sustainable forests. The logging and manufacturing
processes are expected to conform to the environmental regulations of the country of
origin.

John Murray (Publishers)
338 Euston Road
London NW1 3BH

www.johnmurray.co.uk

The authorised representative in the EEA is Hachette Ireland, 8 Castlecourt
Centre, Dublin 15, D15 XTP3, Ireland (email: info@hbgi.ie)

Contents

List of Illustrations

Author's Note

Tintin first appeared in black-and-white, in the magazine *Petit Vingtième*, between 1929 and 1940. Thereafter he moved to the newspaper *Le Soir* until 1944. These strips were packaged up into books, initially by the *Petit Vingtième* itself, and thereafter by the publisher Casterman. From 1942, all Tintin books were published in colour, and most of the old black-and-white stories were coloured and shortened to fit the new format. From 1946, Tintin appeared in his own *Tintin* magazine, and all stories were illustrated in colour from the start.

All Tintin books referred to in the text are the English-language editions, published by Methuen, with the exception of *Tintin In The Land Of The Soviets* and *Tintin And Alph-Art*, both of which are published by Sundancer. A full list of all Tintin titles, together with the dates of their first appearances in magazine, book and translated form, is to be found at the back of this book.

All quotations from Hergé, unless otherwise stated, are drawn from the only major interview he ever gave:

Entretiens Avec Hergé, by Numa Sadoul (Casterman). All quotations from Bob de Moor, Leslie Lonsdale-Cooper and Michael Turner, unless otherwise stated, are drawn from a series of interviews conducted by the author in England and Belgium between December 1988 and October 1990.

This book has been prepared without the assistance of the Hergé Foundation. Certain contributors have asked to remain anonymous.

I

Tintin Keeps Up Appearances

On Thursday 8 May 1930, the train from Moscow pulled into Brussels' Gare du Nord. Station officials fought to control a huge and excited crowd that surged forward, eager to catch a glimpse of their hero. As the big black engine drew to a halt, the carriage doors opened and a familiar quiff was spotted bobbing above the heads of the travellers. The crowd went wild.

The young boy stepping confidently from the train was dressed in Russian costume, as befitting anyone who had just single-handedly conquered an entire continent, and put a nation of cowardly Bolsheviks to flight. By his side strode a small white dog on a lead. Behind him hovered a thin, nervous young man in a raincoat, recognised by only a few as the artist Georges Remi, or 'Hergé', who had spent the past year-and-a-half chronicling the adventures of the lad in front of him for the readers of the *Vingtième Siècle* newspaper. Tintin, junior reporter and adventurer extraordinaire, was coming home to meet his public at last.

The adulation was so unstinting that few onlookers noticed the unusually dark colour of Tintin's hair, or the fact that his quiff kept falling down into his eyes. Doubtless, those that had spotted the sizeable jar of hair grease under Hergé's arm didn't mind that ever-increasing dollops were needed to maintain their hero's celebrated hairstyle. As for the usually perky Snowy, well, the doleful black-eared beagle at Tintin's side simply got lost in a forest of feet. If you'd told the multitude that 'Tintin' was in fact Henri de Donckers, a cut-price actor rented for the day, who'd got on the train with Hergé a couple of stops up the line, none of them would have believed you.

Waiting to meet the train, and Hergé in particular, was an appropriately royalist dignitary – the ex-Empress Zita of Austria-Hungary. Just as the breathless author had made contact with her, and was waiting to be presented officially, the crowd swept Donckers off in another direction. Georges looked at the Empress, at the sagging quiff now disappearing rapidly into the scrum, and at the pot of hair grease in his arms. He made up his mind, and plunged into the crowd after his protégé. For the rest of his life, through thick and thin, euphoria and black depression, he was never able to leave Tintin's side again.

In due course, the prototype comic strip hero the young author had created went on to be massively influential, both commercially and artistically. Inside Hergé's profession, Tintin gave rise to a whole movement, the *bande dessinée* tradition, a style of comic illustration – as distinct from cartooning – that captured the imagination of the European mainland. Many major *bande dessinée* artists were inspired in the first instance by Tintin. Clare

Bretécher, who produced an 'ode to Tintin' on Hergé's death, recalls: 'I was wholly nurtured on Tintin, like all my generation.'[1] Jacques Martin, the creator of *Alix*, who later joined Hergé's staff, remembers: 'I think it was somewhere between *The Broken Ear* and *The Black Island* that I decided to become a comic strip artist . . . I imagined Hergé as a sort of kindly grandfather.'

In the wider public arena, Tintin's success over the intervening years has been no less dramatic. By 1990, over a hundred million Tintin books have been sold. It is an astonishing figure, unmatched outside the enormous markets of the USA. The sales graph resembles the floor of a valley which rises slowly and ever more steeply towards a vertical cliff face. Today, Tintin books are selling as never before, with at least as many adult buyers as children. What is the incredible worldwide appeal of a boy with a 1930s hairstyle, who fights 1930s villains, in 1930s cars, without once disturbing his immaculate 1930s plus fours?

The Belgian critic and intellectual Michel Serres is in no doubt. 'The blank domino generates and embraces the whole series of dominos. The creative centre, Tintin's head or Georges' genius, shine incandescent like the snow on the glaciers of Tibet. Thirty rays, the whole world, Asia, America, the Pacific Islands, Incas, Indians and Congolese, converge upon the hub, which alone gives to the wheel cohesion and fullness, existence and perfection, the empty and transparent circle of the middle, the ingenuous centre, Tintin's head, Georges' angelic soul, air under the feet of Blessed Thunder, ice flow, childhood, everything that says yes.'[2]

There, perhaps, in one paragraph, is the essence of Tintin's success. Hergé detested that sort of pseudo-intellectual rubbish and all who traded in it, and kept his stories as far away from it as possible. The hidden meanings and allegories that others found in Tintin's activities were of no interest to him. His aim was always to keep it simple and direct. Hergé always preferred an illustration that advanced the storyline to one with purely aesthetic appeal.

Whether by accident or design, this narrative directness successfully transcended the boundaries of time and place, and continues to do so. It barely seems to matter today that Tintin's escapades in Eastern Europe in *King Ottokar's Sceptre* are directed at saving the throne of a jodhpur-wearing King from an adversary who sports a monocle and a haircut that went out with the Nuremberg trials. It is hardly important that all the streets in *The Red Sea Sharks* are painstaking observations of obscure parts of Brussels. The stories – and just as importantly, the humour – are universal.

Hergé's jokes, although they developed from simple slapstick in the early days to sophisticated character comedy in later years, were mainly visual. This was not a premeditated bid for international success; it was not until after the war that Tintin escaped the confines of the French- and Flemish-speaking worlds. Right from his earliest and most parochial pre-Tintin material, Hergé always found universal human moods and responses – anger, embarrassment, pomposity, and so on – funnier than any humorous contrivance. He disliked wordplay, pointing to Asterix (perhaps with a modicum of professional jealousy) as an example of how not to do it.

Another aspect of Hergé's character which coincidentally matched the requirements of an international audience was his need to find an escape from the pressures of everyday life. The Tintin stories took their author out of the stultifying boredom of Brussels and away from the stifling weight of Catholic morality and 'civilised' standards that bore down on a small child in turn-of-the-century Belgium. This youthful desire – to travel the world from behind a desk – never left the adult Hergé. He was always trying to escape. In the end, he found himself trying to escape from Tintin as well.

In the first instance, though, the success of Tintin in 1929–30 was tied to a specific innovation. People in Belgium had never actually seen speech bubbles before – they were a new American idea, and Hergé virtually pioneered their use in Europe. The effect was almost seismic. Readers reacted to the early words and deeds of Tintin as if they were carved on tablets of stone.

Looking back now, the adventures that inspired such excitement, such as *Tintin In America, Tintin In The Congo* and *Tintin In The Land Of The Soviets* itself, seem almost slipshod. They are plot-free, happy-go-lucky adventures, a stream of unrelated gags and cliffhangers composed at a time of jollity and youthful exuberance, by inky-fingered juniors in a newspaper office. Little thought went into them – it was too exciting a time for that. Today they are lauded for their primitive artistry, but at the time their readers were not too deeply concerned with the significance of Hergé's emerging clarity of line. The boy reporter was bringing the world to life in their living rooms.

Who cared if the first stories were cheap right-wing propaganda, instigated and directed at small children by a Catholic newspaper editor who kept a framed photograph of Mussolini on his desk? Hergé certainly didn't. When he started Tintin he was still a naive young man who knew little of the world, intelligent, but socially immature like so many of his contemporaries. The early Tintin reflects essentially childish concerns; in particular, the influence of the boy scouts, and the Red Indian games they played, is strongly present. Today the idea of boy scouts in copious shorts and enormous hats being encouraged by adults to pretend to be Red Indians right up to their twentieth birthdays is somewhat laughable, but inter-war Belgium was an innocent place. Scouting was the only escape from the boredom of life at home, and life at home had a habit of dragging on right to the end of one's teens.

Although the Tintin series later developed into a vehicle for knowledgeable satire and sophisticated character comedy, the memory of his baggy shorts never left Hergé. As late as the 1930s he was to correct the unpunctuality of Eugène Evany, a colleague on the *Vingtième Siècle* and later chief of the Hergé Studios, by appealing to his 'scouting spirit'. Tintin was essentially a big boy scout too, he just happened to begin life fighting socialists for a living. Of course, as the 1930s went on, Hergé quickly became powerful and aware enough to divest himself of this right-wing gimmickry, and institute the Tintin we know today, quiff bristling apolitically at the side of the underdog. Enough mud had stuck to cause problems later, but in the sheltered pre-war climate such worries were far away.

True greatness, ground-breaking political satire and major artistic achievement arrived for Hergé and Tintin only when the international upheavals of the 1930s began to impinge upon Belgium's closed society. As war drew nearer, especially, Hergé found himself forced into a long, slow, painful divorce from his youth and from his creation. Put simply, before the war Tintin *was* Hergé, or at least a vehicle for fulfilling his and every boy's fantasies. After the war Hergé identified increasingly with his new character Captain Haddock, a recluse ever in search of the quiet life, free from parrots, opera singers, insurance salesmen, and other irritations of a rich man's world. Tintin himself, although still occupying the leading role, ceased to be the focus for humour and became just one of a much richer family of characters than before.

In part, this was due to Hergé growing up; specific problems had arisen during the war, when Hergé had to learn the hard way that he was not the Tintin type. Other Belgians – the true Tintins of this world – had joined the resistance, blown up railway lines, smuggled escaped P.O.W.s out of the country, and probably would have taken to the hills if there had been any to take to. Hergé, peaceful, cynical, expedient, had obeyed the appeals of the Belgian King and carried on working under the Nazis. Resolutely apolitically of course – not a whiff of partisanship entered the Tintin books during the war years – but the accusations of collaboration were to dog him for the rest of his life. There is an element of stubbornness in the way that he almost refused to defend himself, preferring to retain his dignity, as he perceived it, rather than stoop to debate the issue.

In the short term, the liberation found him in and out of jail and unable to work, a fate not shared by all the thousands of machinists, plumbers and bakers who had carried on working. To rescue himself from what he saw as an iniquitous situation, he had to sell the long-term rights to his own work to the publisher Raymond Leblanc, a pre-war Hergé fan and resistance hero, who had spent the war behaving exactly as Tintin would have done.

The irony could not have been lost on Hergé. Shorn of his independence, the will to work ebbed away. He took to disappearing without warning for long periods. Persuaded back to work by Leblanc, he developed psychosomatic illnesses. Eczema crippled his hands when he tried to draw. He suffered nightmares, and his marriage broke up. Michael Turner, Hergé's friend and co-translator of the Tintin books into English (with Leslie Lonsdale-Cooper), explains: 'One of the things that never comes out is the amount of pressure put on Hergé by the business people. Some of them were quite good friends, but at times they did exploit him a great deal.'

Yet throughout this period, Hergé was drawing his finest work, starting with *Prisoners Of The Sun* in 1948. His great masterpieces of comic art – *The Calculus Affair, Tintin In Tibet, The Castafiore Emerald* – were all inspired, directly or indirectly, by great personal unhappiness.

There were long delays between stories, and during stories, while Hergé became ill or disappeared on his own; but when he worked, he threw himself into his drawings with a venomous perfectionism, creating ferociously detailed and quite brilliant works of art. His personal feelings rarely emerged at work, by his own admission. To his assistants he remained a figure to admire: an affable, witty, generous, talented, helpful man, engagingly vulnerable to office practical jokes. Only a tendency to play the martinet in matters of inefficiency hinted at his inner drive to find whatever it was that was eluding him – independence? Artistic perfectionism? Freedom from responsibility?

Increasingly, Hergé attempted to articulate these personal strivings through his Tintin stories. Most remarkable is *Tintin In Tibet*, a book in which he divested himself of the Tintin family, drew out his nightmares and exorcised them in a personal quest for Chang, the young Chinese boy who had once been his closest and most influential friend. Such nostalgic symbols were vital to Hergé – his later years were peppered with attempts to recreate significant moments from his early life. Like most people's attempts at reliving a supposedly happier past, these seem to have ended in disappointment.

Ultimately, Tintin became an obstacle, not a means, to happiness. Hergé went through periods of hatred for him. In his last completed story, *Tintin And The Picaros* – a critical failure – he toyed listlessly with his characters. Sometimes, at work, he would draw Tintin standing over him with a whip, or ready to hang him with a noose, a cruel expression distorting the little reporter's features. The pictures were funny, but they were disturbing too. Whenever Hergé tried to draw Tintin now, his hands became racked with pain. He told Michael Turner on one occasion, 'I've fallen out of love with Tintin. I just can't bear to see him.'

Instead of working, Hergé left his studios in the hands of his subordinates and went travelling; not for inspiration, but for escape. Tintin could go hang, and so could the final Tintin adventure, which never saw the light of day. Hergé left his creation on page 42 of *Tintin And Alph'Art*, about to be coated in liquid polyester, turned into a work of art, signed by César, authenticated by Zolotas, and then have a long article written about him by Michel Serres. Which is where Tintin was left for ever when, on 4 March 1983, Hergé died of anaemia.

In seventy-six years, Georges Remi had created possibly the greatest comic strip ever seen, pioneered an art form, chronicled history, acquired millions of fans and piles of money, and had come up with some terrific jokes. True, in some respects, the story of Tintin is a sad story; but it also manages to be funny, revealing and dramatic by turns. For lovers of happy endings, it has one of those too. It all starts in Brussels in 1907, in one of the dullest districts it is possible to imagine anywhere . . .

2
Hergé And The Unbelievably Dull Childhood

Some of the most elegant residential districts ever designed employ constant repetition of the same features as part of their appeal. Then there are those districts where a uniformity of design imposes a uniformity of attitude, depressing and limited in scope. Etterbeek in Brussels is one of the latter, a good, solid, Roman Catholic suburb that in the early part of the century took pride in its lack of excitement. Hergé's upbringing was steeped in Catholicism, not a Catholicism to be exploited in the manner of Graham Greene or Evelyn Waugh, but one to be given the slip at the earliest possible opportunity. Of course, he never quite managed this, and his religion continued to influence his life and work indirectly.

Since the age of one, the young Georges Remi had lived in the Rue de Theux with his family. In 1912 they had had the initiative and imagination to move away, but six months later they were back, tails between their legs, albeit some ten doors nearer to the posher end of the street. Georges himself had a gloomy, round-windowed attic bedroom, perhaps similar to that on page 54 of *The Castafiore Emerald*.

Georges' brother, Paul, was an active young boy with a round face and a quiff. His father, Alexis, was a clumsy man with a twin brother, Léon, who lived nearby. The two of them would go for walks, wearing identical bowler hats and carrying identical canes, singing in unison. Sometimes on Sundays, if there was a suspicion anyone might possibly be enjoying themselves, the whole family would descend upon Aunt Ninie, who lived locally too. She would then force them to listen to ear-splitting renderings of songs at the piano, setting glasses quivering and endangering those of her relatives with suspect constitutions.

In later life, Hergé was quick to dismiss as a coincidence any suggestion that Tintin, the Thompson twins, and Bianca Castafiore, his regular pre-war characters, might in any way be connected with this family group. It might also be worth noting, however, that Georges Remi was unusual amongst his schoolfriends in that he had a girlfriend. This precociously ample-breasted object of lust was called Milou, which was the original name he chose to give Tintin's dog Snowy.

This is not actually as bizarre as it sounds. In Belgium at this time, consorting with the opposite sex was considered the sort of crime that would have the Pope revolving in his bed at night. Eventually Georges was sent down from college for inviting some village girls to a barndance. Steeped as he was in this childhood view of morality, even as late as 1929, it would have been unthinkable to provide Tintin with a female companion. What would they do at night on an expedition to the mountains? So, Milou became a dog instead.

Besides, you didn't get any girls in the boy scouts, and that was where the attitudes that characterise Tintin were instilled in Georges Remi. He had first discovered the joys of scouting in 1919, at the age of 12, when he joined the local branch of the 'Scouts de Belgique'. Its appeal was straightforward: whole afternoons, sometimes several days at an end, were spent going off to the countryside, pretending to be Red Indians. The Belgian incarnation of the Baden–Powell scouts had adopted an idealised version of the Red Indian lifestyle almost as its modus operandi. For Georges, as for so many other Belgian children, scouting – and Red Indian games in particular – became synonymous with escape from the dullness of everyday life.

The scouting philosophy, of working and smiling your way through problems rather than fretting over them, never left Hergé. At the crisis period of *Tintin In Tibet*, this reserve of artificial optimism was to prove substantially more successful than psychoanalysis. 'I never cease to be a boy scout,' said Hergé. 'Scouts have never had a good press, and you can understand why. It has its infantile side. But for me it was a good schooling.'

Georges was an intelligent child, bright enough to be frustrated into bad behaviour by his inactivity. The traditional remedy of thrashing an infant within an inch of its life had the drawback of being rather noisy, so – with admirable if unwitting foresight – his parents gave him pen and paper to shut him up. When he joined the boy scout movement, Georges became the unofficial artist of the local troop, and was soon getting his drawings accepted by the local scout magazine *Jamais Assez* ('Never Enough').

After a couple of years, however, the Red Indian idyll came to an abrupt end. Some minor local dignitary, of the big-fish-in-extremely-small-puddle variety, had a word with Georges' parents about the suitability or otherwise of the boy's education. Surely he would be better off in the altogether more wholesome college of St Boniface, and the attendant 'Federation of Catholic Scouts', a religious group which combined the scouting ethic with the spiritual boredom of the Belgian Catholic Church. Mr and Mrs Remi complied, installed Georges at the college forthwith, and in the new scout troop soon afterwards.

Life with the St Boniface scouts was altogether different. To start with, the troop was run by the type of scoutmaster who these days keeps tabloid journalists in work. The sort who believes that small boys are improved by 'discipline', which in this instance meant trapping angry horseflies under a glass on the exposed skin of his youthful charges, and seeing how many bites they could stand. Outside these social get-togethers, the rest of the time was spent – naturally – in starched uniforms, enduring endless religious-cum-military parades. 'I am sure that God does not exist,' Georges repeated to himself as a sort of consoling mantra. He soon developed a deep hatred of officialdom and order, which manifests itself clearly in the Tintin stories. His editors sometimes worried about the degree to which Tintin acts as a free spirit, but of course Tintin's independence is one of his major attractions.

Interestingly, Georges never bore a grudge against his parents for exchanging his happiness for an ounce more social status. His mother, Lisa, whom he didn't get on with anyway, went mad and died soon after the war, but his father Alexis stayed on as his son's business manager for the rest of his life. Nor did he bear a grudge against the scout movement – the true, Baden-Powell version, which he felt had been perverted by its ecclesiastical equivalent. Instead, he did his damnedest to infiltrate the Red Indian ethic into the scouts of St Boniface. Also, he continued to draw, and in February 1922 his work was accepted by the national boy scout magazine.

His parents and his teachers were not impressed. His father, who as a draper had taught him to draw clothes, wished Georges could do something constructive like his brother Paul, who was all set to join the army. (In fact Paul's army life was made a misery upon the success of Tintin, when the source of Hergé's visual inspiration became clear to his fellow officers.) Milou's parents, even less impressed with Georges' desire to become a professional artist, told him to clear off in no uncertain terms – perhaps accounting for Georges' canine revenge later on. His teachers remained resolutely uninterested because, despite plenty of practice in the margins of his textbooks, the one subject the otherwise brilliant lad could not manage at school was art. In later years the famous Hergé ascribed this failing to an unwillingness to undertake tedious drawing exercises – all those doric capitals and so forth – but the fact remains that the young Georges was stylish but far from technically proficient. Over the years he taught himself to an exceptional degree of technical skill, but in the early 1920s he was still only a promising amateur illustrator.

When he did become famous, incredibly rich, and a celebrated artist to boot, he bumped into his former teacher from St Boniface, who asked him, 'And are you still doing those little sketches of yours?' The kind of casual, throwaway remark that conceals years of bitterness, envy, inadequacy and dislike. Georges had not been considered a model pupil, despite his academic achievements, but rather a corrupting influence. In later years, he recounted the story of how, as a child, he had come upon the body of a man who had hanged himself in a wood. Rather than rushing to the church to say prayers for the sinner's soul, he had cut several yards of washing line into small pieces and sold them off in the playground as 'genuine noose souvenirs'. St Boniface was not sorry to see him go.

To the surprise of just about everybody, Georges' drawing did lead to a proper job, and in due course, to wonderful things. In 1924, he had become bored with initialling his drawings 'G.R.', and decided to invert the letters. 'I was young then, of course, and I intended to keep my own name for the great, serious painting I was going to do later on. "Hergé" was just for a laugh, on the side'.[1] Just for a laugh it may have been, but René Weverbergh, who'd bought his work for *Le Boy Scout* magazine, was also employed by the national newspaper *Le Vingtième Siècle* and was looking for new talent. The young man now calling himself 'Hergé' caught his eye.

3

Totor The Boy Scout

Viewed with some sixty-five years' hindsight, *Le Vingtième Siècle* (or 'Twentieth Century') seems a faintly sinister organisation for anyone to join. A 'Catholic Newspaper For Doctrine And Information', it was strictly run by the Abbé Norbert Wallez, he of the desktop portrait of Mussolini.[1] He was not the sort of person who was to find life very convenient in 1945. One of the paper's foreign correspondents was Léon Degrelle, future leader of the Belgian Fascists, or 'our friend' as the SS were later to put it. The *Vingtième* presses were being used on the side by Degrelle to print his own political pamphlets.

Yet before the imagination digresses into fantasies of jack-booted newspaper editors with monocles screwed into one eye, it should be stressed that the *Vingtième Siècle* office had a rather shabby, homely air. There was nothing very sinister about the presence on the staff of Hergé, or of anyone else for that matter. In Belgian suburbia in the 1920s, patriotism, Catholicism, strict morality, discipline and naivety were so inextricably bound together in everyone's lives that right-wing politics were an almost inevitable by-product. It was a world view shared by everyone, distinguished principally by its complete ignorance of the world. In as far as there was a Fascist element, its main aim was to make the proverbial trains run on time. Wallez himself appears to have been a jolly, kindly man, prone to looking after the local down-and-outs.

Obviously, his views influenced the early Tintin, for such was his intention. Tintin was to be the paper's cub reporter, striding about the world righting wrongs and righting lefts, sticking up for the underdog and looking after those less fortunate than himself. It is a credit to Hergé that within a few years, as he gained a measure of independence and as the true nature of European Fascism revealed itself, he was to use the *Vingtième Siècle* as a platform to attack the Nazis directly, while retaining the sympathetic side of Tintin's nature. This was not only brave in terms of petty office politics, but in a wider sense. Belgium was not exactly a well-defended base from which to attack Hitler. It says something about Nazi stupidity that they actually failed to spot the blatant attacks in *King Ottokar's Sceptre* and *Land Of Black Gold*. That such attacks were made at all by a paper like *Le Vingtième Siècle* also suggests that the Abbé Wallez and his colleagues were beginning to have second thoughts as the 1930s went on.

Back in 1925, though, Hergé was still doing odd jobs in the subscriptions department, or for the photo editor. With his military service coming up – a prospect as unwelcome to him as it was appealing to his brother Paul – there wasn't much point in giving him any great responsibility just yet. He still derived the most satisfaction from drawing for *Le Boy Scout* magazine in his spare time. His more formal illustrations there were often stylish and displayed a precocious artistic ability. When he took care over a line drawing, he could fairly be described as an accomplished illustrator. However, he did not appear to adapt well to working at speed, for his cartoon work at this stage was clumsy by comparison, still fumbling for a coherent style.

None the less, it was a cartoon character that Hergé devised for *Le Boy Scout* magazine in 1926, one who he hoped would revolutionise his job prospects. A brave, resourceful young character, who travelled the globe putting wrongs to right, and who would be instantly recognisable on account of his little quiff and daft baggy trousers. An example for others to follow. In short, a boy scout called Totor.

It was to be three years before Totor metamorphosed into Tintin. In the meantime Hergé took him to the USA, where he enjoyed a series of running escapades with cowboys and Indians, some of which turned up again in *Tintin In America*. He rode sharks, captured gangsters and escaped being scalped by inches, all without once ruffling his copious boy scout shorts, putting one in mind of Tintin's fifty-year devotion to the same pair of plus fours. Like Tintin, he was based on Hergé's own youthful fantasies. Where Hergé had been leader of Squirrel Patrol, Totor was the fearless patrol leader of the Cockchafers; but the essential difference between the two characters lay in the format. Unlike Tintin, Totor didn't speak in bubbles. The pictures didn't move the story along. They merely illustrated a slightly rambling and uninspired text.

There were hints of great things to come, though. Already, Hergé was developing his own peculiar cartoon vocabulary. Little stars or puffs of dust, to indicate an impact. Little droplets, to indicate effort or surprise. Little jagged lines to indicate anger, and at this stage, fear. Lines to indicate speed and movement. Take a look at page 7 of *Flight 714*, the peak of Hergé's artistic achievement forty years later, and the whole shorthand can be seen there, speaking volumes.

According to Hergé, he had been influenced by *The Rainbow*, a British comic he had read during the First World War, but the more important influences were American. Crucially, Léon Degrelle, on assignment in Mexico, had picked up a bundle of US comics and posted them back to the youngster. The new American device of the speech bubble was much in evidence; and a few question marks, exclamation marks and Americanisms in tentative bubbles began to creep into *Totor*. Amongst the bundle of comics was George McManus' *Bringing Up Father*, from which Totor's (and Tintin's) button nose was borrowed. American films played their part too, for the young Hergé still harboured a secret desire to be a film director. He grandly titled the adventures of Totor 'An Extrasuperfilm' or 'A Grand Comic Film', presented by 'Hergé Moving Pictures'. By the time of *Flight 714* his technique was to become almost exclusively cinematic, although the various attempts at filming Tintin never met with success.

After his call-up, Hergé continued to send Totor strips back to what was by now calling itself *Le Boy Scout Belge* magazine, from his unpleasant berth at the first regiment of light infantry. By his own account it was a brutal outfit, that made the scouts of St Boniface and their horsefly practice seem like a nuns' tea party. It was worth the effort, though. On his release in October 1927, he was rewarded with an illustrator's job on *Le Vingtième Siècle*, working principally on the women's pages at first. No doubt in order to familiarise himself with the subject matter in hand, he spent a lot of time chatting up the Abbé's secretary, Germaine Kieckens, a straightforward suburban girl intellectually his inferior, but whose adult manner aroused his interest in a way needing no discussion here. For her part, this lovable, humorous youth brought out the maternal instincts in her. In 1928, Hergé proposed to Germaine, and she accepted.

Then, ominously, towards the end of the year, Wallez himself called Hergé in for an interview. Facing the Abbé across the gleaming portrait of the Duce, Hergé learnt that the Abbé, too, had been scanning the American papers. They had weekly comic supplements, which upped circulation figures and attracted younger readers who might be weaned on to the main paper in due course. Younger readers ripe for introduction to the delights of the Abbé's own political and religious views. He had decided to launch *Le Petit Vingtième* – the 'Little Twentieth' – and was looking for an editor. 'Somebody ought to be getting busy with that, then,' said Hergé. 'Yes, you,' explained the Abbé.[2] 'I was terrified,' recalled Hergé later.[3] Of course, the Abbé went on, the new supplement would need a new strip. Something combining humour, adventure and morality, that would have the kids of Brussels flocking to the news stands every week to buy it. Hergé was to illustrate that strip. Yes! it was to be called *Flup, Nénesse, Poussette & Cochonnet*, and it was to be written by the sports reporter.

It is hard not to spot an element of disillusionment creeping in here. *Flup, Nénesse*, etc wasn't up to much, and the sports reporter was not famed for his versatility (some things haven't changed since the 1920s). In fact, it was little better than *The Travels Of A Little Spider*, illustrated by Hergé and written by the firm's book-keeper a few months before. The Abbé Wallez counted thrift among the virtues of a good newspaper editor, and his generosity certainly did not extend to hiring anyone as wasteful as a specialist children's writer. Come to that, this attitude had a lot to do with Hergé's big break. He was, after all, an assistant in the photo department who drew a little for a boy scout magazine.

For two months from its inception on 1 November 1928, Hergé struggled on with *Le Petit Vingtième*. As with Totor, he threw in the odd American-style bubble and the repertoire of Hergé cartoon symbols, but *Flup, Nénesse, Pousette & Cochonnet* wasn't working. Hergé himself was still coming to terms with the drawing style. His illustrations for the women's section had been elegant and stylised, but essentially formal. Breathing life into the sports reporter's deathless prose was proving a much more difficult task. Totor, meanwhile, continued sporadically at *Le Boy Scout Belge*. Despite the obvious clumsiness with which his adventures were being dashed off, Totor indisputably had a certain appeal that *Flup, Nénesse*, etc lacked. There were clear grounds for change.

At the end of 1928, the editor of *Le Petit Vingtième* announced a new leading character for the children's supplement. In fact, the new character was to be Totor, but with a few alterations. This would be an American-style strip, with no accompanying text. The illustrations themselves would provide the narrative drive, and what speech there was would sit in those all-important bubbles. At school during the First World War, Hergé had drawn the adventures of an unnamed schoolboy hero who fought the Germans. For *Le Boy Scout*, the hero had become a boy scout. At the *Vingtième Siècle*, Hergé's desk was situated by the back door, where the glamorous foreign correspondents dashed in and out with exotic labels on their suitcases. Small wonder, then, that his new newspaper hero was to be a reporter, albeit – as Hergé put it – 'a reporter with the spirit of a boy scout'. The hero's name was Tintin.

4

Tintin In The Land Of The Soviets

Tintin Au Pays Des Soviets

On 4 January 1929, in issue ten of the *Petit Vingtième*, a plump boy in a check suit with plus fours, black socks and an Eton collar was pictured marching along a Moscow street. This was Tintin. As yet, like Totor, the famous quiff remained plastered to his forehead. It was not until a particularly thrilling car chase on page 8[1] that the wind first blew it into its now familiar gravity-defying position. To the Tintin reader of today the figure would be unrecognisable. Snowy, by his side, looks more familiar, although even he sports a curious beard which he combs in front of a mirror on page 138, in preparation for the big homecoming reception.

When the adventure proper began on 10 January, it was to occupy sixteen months and 139 pages of rambling slapstick adventure, with Tintin by turns blown up, dive-bombed, hit by a locomotive and then frozen solid by evil communists. The characters were negligible and there was a complete absence of plot. Hergé was dashing off two pages a week on Wednesdays, between his other duties as editor of the *Petit Vingtième*. The result was usually rather rushed. 'The *Petit Vingtième* came out on Wednesday evening,' he said, 'and I often didn't have a clue on Wednesday morning how I was going to get Tintin out of the predicament I had put him in the previous week.' Fans of the meticulous Hergé style of later years are usually amazed when they first see the slapdash nature of this early artwork. 'I didn't consider it real work,' said Hergé, 'just a game.'

Despite this, it is hard to imagine the sheer public excitement generated by the new character and the new format. Although Alain St Ogan, a French illustrator, had beaten Hergé to the use of the comic strip in Europe, French publishers could not understand *Tintin In The Land Of The Soviets* at all. When it appeared in the French magazine *Coeurs Vaillants* (Stout Hearts) from 1930 onwards, it was initially printed with explanatory subtitles, until Hergé put a stop to the practice. The public loved it though, both French and Belgian. Soon, the circulation of *Le Vingtième Siècle* was shooting up sixfold on Tintin day.

The object of their adulation seemed rather anonymous to be getting such attention. He was almost featureless, ageless, sexless and did not appear to be burdened with a personality. Yet this very anonymity remains the key to Tintin's gigantic international success. With so little to mark him out, anybody from Curaçao to Coventry can identify with him and live out his adventures. Millions have done so, both adults and children, including the likes of Steven Spielberg, Andy Warhol, Wim Wenders, Françoise Sagan, Harold Macmillan and General de Gaulle, who considered Tintin his only international rival. When plans to make

a Tintin film were announced one African boy delighted Hergé by writing in to say he'd be ideal for the
part. One German boy who discovered a burglar in his
house knocked him out, 'because that's what Tintin
would have done'.

This escapist element applied as much to Hergé as it
did to his readers, and never more so than in 1929. 'My
ideal was to be like Tintin,' he confessed, 'a hero
without fear or reproach. Alas! it was an illusion, long
since faded away.' On to these youthful dreams he
grafted the body of his brother, and curiously, the
clothes of a Canadian student at St Boniface called
Charles, who had been laughed at for his plus fours and
Argyll socks. Perhaps, if Hergé had been one of the
laughers, an element of guilt was involved.

The result, incidentally, bore an uncanny resemblance to a character called Tintin–Lutin, created around
1900 by Fred Isly and Benjamin Rabier. (Similarities
have also been claimed to a character called Floridor,
and his dog Carabi, whose adventures were drawn by
Ernest Picard in 1915, but this is more tenuous.) Hergé
did not like admitting to outside influences, but this one
would have been hard to deny: the two creations looked
extremely similar in the trouser–and–hairstyle department, as Hergé was gracious enough to acknowledge.
However, their characters bore no similarities at all.
Tintin–Lutin was an unpleasant Struwwelpeter-type
infant, always getting punished and held up as a moral
warning to little readers. Tintin, on the other hand, had
perhaps too much of the goody-goody about him. He
never misbehaved or laughed at anyone; but at least he

wasn't priggish. Hergé admitted as much, ascribing it to his own Catholic upbringing. 'If Tintin is a moralist, he's a moralist who doesn't take things too seriously, so humour is never far away from his stories.'

Snowy, or Milou,[2] apart from having the name of Hergé's ex-girlfriend, was a fairly conventional talking dog. He and Tintin enjoyed some really quite substantial conversations, especially in the spaces between adventures in the *Petit Vingtième*. He held the position of confidant until the arrival in 1940 of Captain Haddock, who apart from usurping his place as Tintin's No.1 friend, seems to have robbed Snowy of the power of speech. This is a reflection of Hergé's developing realism (virtually absent in the Russian adventure) and also of his gradual departure from the Tintin persona.

As the years went by, Tintin stories were written more and more for the adult Hergé and his adult audience, as well as for his younger readers. Hergé liked the analogy of a Neapolitan cake, 'with a slice for the children, a slice for adolescents, another one for grown-ups and then a slice for the specialist'. Back in the early days, though, he was aiming principally at children. 'The adults are nearly all ridiculous, did you notice? But Tintin never is. Perhaps this satisfies the children's taste for revenge.'[3]

Even so, *Tintin In The Land Of The Soviets* does contain the occasional sly wink to the grown-ups. The cloth-capped party of English communists that visits the Soviet factory on page 26, for instance, is out-and-out adult parody. A few pages later, the factory in question turns out to be an empty shell, with Soviet agents burning straw and beating sheet metal to create an appearance of industrial prosperity. This was the influence of the Abbé Wallez creeping in. 'That's how the Soviets fool the poor idiots who still believe in a "red paradise",' explains Tintin. Wallez had given Hergé a book called *Moscow Unveiled*, the thrust of which is not difficult to guess, with orders to digest and pass on the information therein to the impressionable young readers of the *Petit Vingtième*. Great unexpurgated chunks of it were to be regurgitated by Tintin during the course of the adventure.

Moscow Unveiled was the work of Joseph Douillet, a Catholic diplomat who had risen to the giddy heights of Belgian consul in Rostov-on-Don, and who violently disapproved of everything Russian from vodka to co-education. While Douillet had undoubtedly witnessed some of the true horrors of early Stalinism during his travels, he was not one to subjugate prejudice to facts. The shock-horror tone with which all things from famine to rigged elections are revealed contains an air of hysteria entirely inappropriate to the knockabout thrills of *Tintin In The Land Of The Soviets*.

None the less, the story caught the rabidly anti-communist mood of the average Belgian parent perfectly. Most of the populace genuinely believed that all Russians were grinning devils with knives between their teeth, who butchered small children for kicks. Anyone like Tintin who could land a right cross on a Russian or two, or twenty, had to be a good sort. 'Anything Bolshevik was atheist,'[4] explained Hergé simply. To Belgian Catholics, this was justification enough.

In later years Hergé was to find the entire story profoundly embarrassing, and referred to it as 'a transgression of my youth' which had arisen because he knew no better. He always refused to allow its republication, although the enormous proliferation of pirate editions forced him to go ahead with a facsimile version in 1973. The book was never modernised or coloured, and it was to be sixty years before its appearance in the English language.

Wallez, though, was delighted at the transformation Tintin had made to his paper. He began to take on a paternalistic attitude to the boy reporter. It was he who dreamed up and arranged the staged 'return' from Moscow by train, and he who had the bright idea of issuing the story in book form. He also urged Hergé to invent new characters, and on 23 January 1930 two street urchins named Quick and Flupke appeared, whose adventures were to run side by side with Tintin's for the next eleven years. Like Tintin, Quick and Flupke fleshed out another adolescent fantasy – that of childish misbehaviour. They roamed the streets of Etterbeek getting up to the kind of pranks the religious scouts would have never tolerated in Hergé. Unlike Tintin, however, the pair never graduated from the staple diet of slapstick gags dreamed up on the morning of publication. Today, their trail of irate policemen and crashed go-karts seems charmingly dated.

One famous criticism of Tintin, often ascribed to this youthful lack of realism on Hergé's part, is that he is not much of a reporter. He never phones in his copy or consults his editor about deadlines, and he seems to exist on especially lavish expenses. In actual fact, Tintin does more reporting *In The Land Of The Soviets* than in any other adventure. On page 35, after a hard day's work biffing commissars, he posts off an enormous article exposing corruption in Soviet local elections. Such criticisms, though, rather miss the point of Tintin's job.

During the 1920s there had been a great fashion for adventurer–journalists, who created their own news and reported it from a very personal perspective, forty years before the 'me' generation. The trend, set by reckless, often roguish characters such as Albert Londres, Joseph Kessel and Henri de Monfreid, had certainly filtered down as far as *Le Vingtième Siècle*. At one stage, when Hergé had enquired about a reporter's job, he had been told that 'a true reporter never asks what he should report'. The adventures of Tintin, then, *were* his copy. He was creating news out in Russia by upsetting the system, and filing that news back in the shape of a cartoon strip.

Tintin went on reporting quite overtly until the war, when the German occupation made any sort of journalism dangerous to portray. There is plenty of journalistic activity in the early part of *Land Of Black Gold*, for instance, where Tintin conducts a lengthy interview with a petrol company boss. After the German invasion, however, journalists changed their spots. A reporter was someone who swallowed the party line whole, as fed to him by the authorities, so Tintin became a reporter in name only.

That, in short, is the sole potentially damaging criticism to be levelled at the activities of Tintin in Russia:

that Hergé did what he was told by the Abbé Wallez. The official line of the Hergé Foundation nowadays is to ascribe this to naiveté, but Hergé himself always emphasised that it was impossible for anyone from his background not to assimilate right-wing views to some extent. That, together with the quite understandable expediency of a young author who had found a rich seam, and was temporarily prepared to compromise his principles in order to be allowed to continue exploiting it, made *Tintin In The Land Of The Soviets* susceptible to propaganda influences. Essentially, Hergé was biding his time.

Hergé's own beliefs leaned to the right only in that it seemed more logical and functional to him to improve existing conditions by making them succeed on their own terms, rather than by the wholesale application of predetermined and possibly inappropriate left-wing ideology. He certainly did not lean as far right as the views expressed in *Soviets*, and planned to swing his next adventure in the opposite direction. He would take Tintin to the USA, and highlight the plight of the Red Indian faced with the encroachments of modern America. Despite the dash of scouting romanticism, this was too much for the Abbé Wallez, whose idea of the noble savage was as someone to be tamed, rather than encouraged. A major disagreement loomed.

5

Tintin In The Congo

Tintin Au Congo

A burly rhinoceros lumbers gracefully into the shade of a tree, seeking refuge from the African sun. From the branches, two hands reach down, holding a drill, and proceed to bore a hole in the animal's armoured hide. Then, a thin stick of dynamite is lodged under the rhinoceros' skin. A few seconds to lay the fusewire and get clear, and the mighty beast is blown to smithereens. Tintin, amateur naturalist, is at work again.

Tintin In The Congo is best described as another youthful transgression. At least, that is how an embarrassed Hergé later wrote it off. 'For *Tintin In The Congo*, the fact is that I was fed on the prejudices of the bourgeois society I lived in. It was 1930. The only things I knew about these countries were what people said about them at the time. Africans were no more than big children. "It's lucky for them that we're over there," and so on. I drew Africans along these lines in the purely paternalistic spirit of the times in Belgium.'

In November 1988, Sue Buswell, then editor of Tintin at Hergé's British publishers Methuen, put it more succinctly to the *Mail On Sunday* newspaper:

'Basically, it's all to do with rubbery lips and heaps of dead animals.'[1] Whether or not this was taken out of context – the newspaper was trying to mount a shock-horror exposé of Tintin's true nature some sixty years too late – it's a fairly apt summary.

Hergé had lost his battle with the Abbé Wallez. In a few years, he would be strong enough to get his own way, but for the time being the Abbé was firm about what he wanted. The little readers of the *Petit Vingtième* were to get a lesson in the virtues of colonialism. Tintin was to bring enlightenment to the natives and honourable death to the wildlife of the Belgian Congo, 'our beautiful colony which has such great need of us, tarantara, tarantaboom', as Hergé sarcastically reported the conversation.

This was not just conventional right-wing propaganda on the Abbé's part. Wallez had a vision of a strong, united European alliance (a man ahead of his time?) which would counterbalance the power of the United States and the British Empire, and he wished to inculcate it in his readership at an impressionable age. Certainly, some of his theories rubbed off on Hergé, if subconsciously. The original version of *The Shooting Star* features a pan-European party of scientists in a victorious race against villainous American opposition. Hergé's moonshot lifted off from Europe rather than America. Also, a surprising number of Hergé's baddies were British or American. Rastapopoulos was American-Greek; Captain Allan was British; many of the baddies in *The Blue Lotus* and *The Broken Ear* were British or American; Tintin beats up three British soldiers in the original *Lotus;* and until Hergé's British editors requested a re-write, *Land Of Black Gold* was extremely uncomplimentary about the post-war British regime in Palestine. To some extent Hergé's Anglo-American baddies must have derived from imported US films, whereas his hero was naturally a homegrown Belgian boy; yet there is no doubt that Wallez's vision of Europe thoroughly permeates the Tintin canon, starting at its most basic form with *Tintin In The Congo.*

Tintin is seen teaching the merits of Europe to African children in an impromptu geography lesson. 'Today I'm going to teach you about your homeland,' he intones. 'Belgium.' (After the war this was 'modernised', no less patronisingly, to read, 'Now who can tell me what two and two make? . . . Nobody?') His attitude to the natives is patronising in the extreme, and they in turn are depicted as lazy and stupid. Their workmanship is humorously shoddy. When Tintin's car stalls on a railway crossing in the path of an oncoming train, the engine promptly bounces off the car and derails. The rubber-lipped passengers that climb out are far too workshy to restart the locomotive, so Tintin hauls it to the nearest station using his car. Presumably in gratitude for this remarkable ingenuity, four natives immediately start carrying him around on a sedan chair.

Patronising then, but by no means deliberately racist. There are good guys and bad guys both black and white, and Tintin comes to the aid of a native boy (Coco) who has been attacked by wicked whiteys, something that was to become a habit in later stories. Coco is then befriended by Tintin, who drives him around for a while, and one senses Hergé's conscience showing through. His reluctance to draw the story at all shows through equally clearly. *Congo* is almost a regression from *Soviets*, with no plot and precious little characterisation, and is probably the most childish of all the Tintin books.

Hergé's reservations about sending Tintin to the Congo did not, however, have anything to do with a desire to present a true picture of the country. He wouldn't have known a true picture of the country from the Mona Lisa. He didn't even know that the Congolese needed defending from the depredations of their Belgian overseers. His view of them was restricted to that patronising sympathy common to many of his countrymen. The Belgian Congo was one of the most viciously repressive of all colonial regimes, but the Belgians themselves remained utterly ignorant of conditions there until relatively modern times. Hergé's problem was that he simply wasn't interested in the Congo.

Artistically, the Congolese were depicted as caricature black men. Although his more considered illustration work was advancing by leaps and bounds, Hergé was still struggling with the new comic strip medium. He was making the mistake of trying to draw fast and funny pictures to match the fast and funny text, a method which was alien to him. Gradually, as the 1930s progressed, he was to develop the influential 'clear line' style that suited him so well. The essence of the modern Tintin is that only the faces are funny, or caricatured in any way; everything else is faithfully rendered into bold and detailed line illustrations, without the slightest hint of impressionism. It is not cartooning in the accepted sense, but a hybrid between cartooning and illustration, albeit a highly successful hybrid that has spawned hundreds of imitators.

In 1930, the victims of Hergé's early attempts at caricature were the Africans, and in later years Hergé found himself profoundly embarrassed by these drawings. Not that he felt guilty, conditioned as his early work was by his upbringing. What did bother him, looking back, was the wholesale slaughter of African wildlife. Tintin treats the local fauna proprietorially, regarding each horned head as if he were sizing it up for mounting on a shield. Apart from dynamiting rhinos, he deliberately uses a magnifying glass to burn an elephant's head, and in one sequence of high comedy guns down at least ten antelopes with a hunting rifle.

It is cruel, but cruel in a very childlike way. In 1930, Hergé was still writing simplistic stories for kids. Over the next ten years he was to mature at an extraordinary rate, reaching a high level of technical sophistication and developing a far more informed outlook on the world. In particular, he became a fervent opponent of all bloodsports. Only two years later, in *Cigars Of The Pharaoh*, Tintin befriended a herd of elephants, learned their language and went to live with them. As he grew up, Hergé rebelled against the conservative values of his childhood so prevalent in *Congo*. The fact that he waited until his early twenties to stage this teenage rebellion says more about Belgium between the wars than about him, whatever his fiancée might have muttered about late development.

Being a childish story, *Tintin In The Congo* was not unnaturally extremely popular with children. When the strip came to an end on 11 June 1931, the eager Abbé Wallez arranged another home-coming stunt. A month later, another actor (Henri de Donckers had got the sack following the hair grease debacle) arrived in Brussels, this time accompanied by ten Congolese bearers and a menagerie of wild animals hired from a circus. Lions notwithstanding, there was a terrible scuffle as a crowd of five thousand surrounded the newspaper office in the Boulevard Bischoffsheim, demanding their share of an insufficient supply of sweets and African souvenirs. When the process was repeated in Liège, there was a near riot. Wallez was delighted.

As with *Tintin In The Land Of The Soviets*, Hergé was not keen to keep the book on sale in later years, but the continued commercial success of the story won him round. The biggest market of all was in the Belgian Congo, and it continues to sell in great numbers in independent Zaire today. Zairean children, it seems, consider it an honour that Tintin included their country in his list of those meriting a visit. Michael Turner, who was a director of Methuen as well as being Hergé's translator, explains: 'Hergé was always being attacked for being a very bad example for children, but of course the people who are concerned about children often have nothing much to do with children.'

None the less Methuen is one of those publishers which has always steadfastly ignored *Tintin In The Congo*. Tintin publishers in some countries refuse to countenance publishing it at all. Others, like Sweden's

Carlsen, asked Hergé to redraw the more gratuitous sequences, exchanging Tintin's dynamite for a camera. In 1946 Hergé did redraw and colour the story, halving its length to the regulation sixty-two pages and toning down the worst colonialist excesses. Oddly, he chose to insert the Thompson twins in the new opening frame of the book, two books before Tintin actually met them for the first time. Also to be found in the same frame are Quick and Flupke (black beret and striped scarf), Hergé himself (brown jacket and grey trousers), and E. P. Jacobs, the colourist who worked with him on the book (behind Hergé, with bow tie).

Today *Tintin In The Congo* is cautiously emerging into the light of re-acceptance as a historical curiosity. It is possible to assess it intelligently on these terms, just as Hergé did. The present day Tintin establishment sees it rather differently. In 1989 Nick Rodwell, Studio Hergé's then agent in Britain, told *Time Out*[2] magazine of his keenness to publish the work in the UK via his own publishing company. 'Tintin is a reporter, so for example he reports what the Congo was like,' he offered. Printing an English-language version in black-and-white, and not colour, would 'defuse the race issue'. Well, it probably wouldn't need to. Viewed in the appropriate context, *Tintin In The Congo* is no more offensive today than, say, the works of John Buchan.

Among the passages that Hergé cut from the original black-and-white edition was one of Tintin's final speeches. As his biplane lifts off from African soil, Tintin turns to his co-pilot with some relief. 'That's the end of our assignment in the Congo,' he says, 'God knows which part of the world we'll be sent to next, when we get back.' This was a sly dig at the Abbé rather than at God, but it was not necessary. Wallez was so pleased with Tintin's success he was prepared to let Hergé have his own way at last. The same passage, as amended in the later version of the book, is more succinct. 'America is waiting,' says Tintin.

6

Tintin In America

Tintin En Amérique

Although the Abbé Wallez had indeed allowed Hergé to take Tintin to America, he certainly didn't appear to be keen on any nonsense about underprivileged Red Indians. The story he actually agreed to involved Tintin exposing the Chicago Crime Syndicates, and was called *Tintin In Chicago*. At least, that's the title it began under in the *Petit Vingtième*. Small wonder though that Bobby Smiles, the crime boss being hunted by Tintin, flees to the Wild West as early as page 16.[1] It was as good an excuse as any.

Tintin And The Red Indians was the story Hergé actually wanted to write. Not that he did the idea justice with *Tintin In America*. Although it's a great improvement on the old Totor strips he based it on, it still amounts to little more than a tourist ramble round the country. Along with *Soviets* and *Congo*, it might be said to represent Hergé's early period, a phase it brought to an end. British Tintin fans unfamiliar with the first two books will get a good idea of their style from *Tintin In America*, which is only marginally more sophisticated. Hergé himself tacitly acknowledged that he could have done better when, in 1957, he considered taking Tintin back to Red Indian territory, and covering the same ground all over again. In the end, he abandoned the idea as a backward step, which was probably the right decision.

At the time, though, Hergé couldn't get enough of Red Indians, arrows, tomahawks, wigwams, totem poles and the rest. Parallel to *Tintin In America* he drew a short-lived strip for a promotional paper, given away by the 'Innovation' department store in Brussels, called *Tim The Squirrel*. This was obviously inspired by his own scouting days as leader of the Squirrel patrol, when he would lead his scouts on their customary Red Indian escapades. Tim The Squirrel metamorphosed into a bear cub in *The Adventures Of Tom And Millie* in the *Meuse* newspaper, which in turn led to *The Adventures Of Popol And Virginia In The Far West*, back in the *Petit Vingtième* in 1934. A bear in a stetson and big leather trousers rides round the West with his gal bear by his side, getting into scrapes. It wasn't up to much, and Hergé soon lost interest, blaming the limited potential of animal characters.

For his entire life, though, he was to remain fascinated by a mythical world of warpaint and feathers. This is not as adolescent as it sounds, though undoubtedly *Tintin In America* is an adolescent book. For an entire generation of Belgian ex-scouts, the Red Indian world represented the only escape from the pressures and frustrations of everyday life. As late as the post-war 1940s, when Hergé was over forty himself and suffering from a personal and professional crisis, he went into retreat in a monastery with his friend Marcel Dehaye – not for religious reasons, but to set up a Red Indian tent in the grounds and live in it without being disturbed for a while. One of the monks, Père Gall, had been postally adopted by 'Black Elk' of the Ogalalla tribe, who had renamed him 'Lakota Ishnawa', or 'Solitary Sioux'. Gall taught Hergé and Dehaye to smoke a peace pipe. It is an absurd notion – three grown men pretending to be Red Indians in the grounds of a monastery – but it goes some way to demonstrating the hold that Red Indian culture had over Hergé and his contemporaries.

In many ways, the Abbé Wallez personified everything that the Red Indians represented an escape from. It was probably for his benefit that the Indians in *Tintin In America* are presented as threatening, at least until it becomes clear that they are used to rough treatment from white men. In publishing terms at least, sympathy with Red Indians was a revolutionary attitude in 1931; and it was fortunate for Hergé that his distaste for the American business interests which were driving the Indians from their land coincided with the Abbé's own fear of America and its dissolute ways. The almost surreal scene on page 29,[2] where oil is discovered on Indian land, businessmen move in, and a huge city is constructed within twenty-four hours, is the highlight of the book. It is echoed, to some extent, by a nice little vignette on page 44,[3] where Tintin – having finally brought Bobby Smiles to justice – is surrounded by men in trilby hats waving wads of money: 'Ten thousand dollars for Snowy's picture on our Doggie Dinners: "I win the tricks with Bonzo Bix, says super-sleuth

Snowy!".' The original *Petit Vingtième* version was not quite so witty, but social comment was burgeoning amid the thrills and spills.

The oil exploitation scene, unfortunately, presaged more than just an intelligent new ingredient in the Tintin stories. It also sowed the seeds of a long-running and unseemly relationship between Hergé and various American editors. Perhaps because of the vague under-current of anti-Americanism that ran through the Tintin books, and certainly because of scenes such as the one outlined above, Hergé's work was never treated with the reverence accorded it by European publishers.

The Americans put themselves firmly in the wrong when they refused to print any frames that pictured black people at all. Outrageously, as late as the 1960s, Hergé was forced to go over parts of his work and remove black characters. The doorman at the half-built bank in this same scene was originally black, as were the mother and baby whom Tintin inadvertently disturbs on page 47.[4] Like *Tintin In The Congo* (which needless to say was ruled right out of court), *Tintin In America* had been shortened, re-drawn and coloured in 1946; but a close look at the frame in question shows that it is a later insert. Compared to the other drawings on page 47, the thickness of line and colouring are different.

To this day, America is the one major market Hergé never cracked, probably because although Tintin was inspired by an American comic strip tradition, he doesn't actually fit into it. US cartoons have always been tied to serial publication in newspapers, in magazines, with exploitation on a massive scale. By the time Tintin was big enough to attract the attention of American publishers, Hergé was neither interested nor prolific enough to join in the circus. For their part the Americans, says Michael Turner, 'hadn't the faintest idea what property they had, and the Golden Press canned it after about two years.' Fortunately, since the 1970s, Tintin has been published in the US by the relatively sympathetic firm of Atlantic–Little Brown.

Back in Belgium, of course, *Tintin In America* was taking Hergé to new heights of popularity. On the professional side, commissions were flooding in. He found himself drawing still more strips – *The Amiable Mr Mops* and the bizarrely titled *Misadventures Of Jeff de Bakker And Dropsy* – together with a number of advertising commissions. His eventual solution was to found the *Atelier Hergé*, a sort of homegrown studio, which died out when it became clear that he was wildly overreaching himself. In the public arena, *America* was the most popular adventure so far. The biggest crowd yet turned up to the third of the Abbé's faked 'homecomings'. Another huge crowd invaded Hergé's wedding to Germaine, which was presided over by Wallez. She still thought Hergé a touch juvenile, but then, what did she expect from a man who listed *Robinson Crusoe, Treasure Island* and *The Three Musketeers* among his ten favourite books?

In part, Tintin's increasing popularity can be attributed to public familiarity with his adventures, but even two years into the Tintin series the medium itself continued to provide tremendous excitement. Despite Hergé's self-consciously comic drawings, an air of

realism still hung about Tintin's travels, which was revi-
talised in *Tintin In America* by the inclusion of a real
character. Al Capone, the gangland boss who was very
much alive and well in 1931, gets arrested and tied up by
Tintin on page 7 of the story.[5] (Sadly, he had to escape
for obvious historical reasons, and Tintin had to content
himself with arresting a mere 355 members of the nebu-
lous Central Syndicate Of Chicago Gangsters instead.)
Capone's activities were famous enough for him to start
passing into legend during his lifetime, and thereafter
into fiction, although what he thought of *Tintin In
America* is not recorded. Presumably he never read it, as
evidenced by the fact that nobody ever found Hergé
floating face down in a canal.

As with *Tintin In The Land Of The Soviets*, Hergé had
obtained most of his facts about Chicago and its gangsters from one book – in this instance *Scenes From Future
Life* by Georges Duhamel – although he had initially
been inspired by an article in the oddly named *Le
Crapouillot* (Mortar Bomb) magazine. Amongst other
things, Duhamel's exposé of the city provided him with
the idea for the gruesome abattoir scene at the end of
the book, where Tintin returns to Chicago only to end
up in a meat pie production line. Assuming that Hergé's
working methods had not changed over the previous
two years, the unexpected strike that saves him would
have been the product of one of the author's celebrated
Wednesday morning panic sessions.

For all its lack of flow and inclusion of such last-
minute ideas, *Tintin In America* does contain pointers to
greater things. Characters stick around for longer,

including Hergé's first humorous character, the abysmal detective (and forerunner of the Thompsons) Mike MacAdam. Glimpsed at the bottom of page 57[6] is a prototype Rastapopoulos, the film producer who was to become Tintin's principal adversary the following year. Snowy's role as talking dog is in the process of being taken down a peg: the book contains the last conversation where Tintin directly understands his words. Hergé is using more imagination in his visual composition; the large drawing of Tintin on a skyscraper window ledge on page 10 is – even in the original[7] – an impressive development. So successful were the stories becoming that the huge Franco–Belgian publisher Casterman took over publication of the book versions from *Le Vingtième Siècle*, and money started to come in.

Yet there was still an ingredient missing – something that would revolutionise the Tintin stories and turn them into works of brilliance. In 1932, it transpired, that extra something was just around the corner.

7

Cigars Of The Pharaoh

Les Cigares Du Pharaon

After successful trips to northerly climes (Russia), the Wild West (America) and the far south (the Congo), it came as little surprise when Tintin's fourth adventure began on 8 December 1932 under the title *Tintin In The East*. It was to be an extra-large double-sized adventure, later split by Hergé into two books. Sometime between the story getting underway in the magazine and its appearance in book form, Hergé got bored with 'Tintin In . . .' titles, and opted for the enigmatic instead. Hence *Cigars Of The Pharaoh* and *The Blue Lotus*.

The new-style titles were the least of the changes that suddenly overwhelmed the adventures of Tintin. *Cigars Of The Pharaoh* is almost completely unrecognisable from its predecessors. Almost overnight, Tintin had become pacy, witty, stylish, mysterious. The further changes that elevated *The Blue Lotus* to new heights are well documented, but the influence brought to bear on the first half of *Tintin In The East* is largely unsung. Conventional wisdom among the gaggle of bearded Tintin scholars that infest Belgium and France even has it that *Cigars Of The Pharaoh* is on a par with its three predecessors. Any true Tintin fan will tell you this is not so. Suddenly, random slapstick had been replaced by beautifully observed character comedy. The book is stuffed with inspired comic characters. Foremost among them, of course, are the Thompson twins, the hopeless detective double act who hamper Tintin's efforts for the rest of his career. At this stage, the pair didn't even have names. In the *Petit Vingtième* version they were known as X-33 and X-33a. Originally, it wasn't until *The Broken Ear* that Thompson uttered the immortal words 'to be precise'[1] before repeating his partner's words with unerring imprecision, and it wasn't until *King Ottokar's Sceptre*, six years later, that Hergé christened them Dupond and Dupont. In English, that translates as Thompson and Thomson, but to the Spaniards they are Hernandez and Fernandez, to the Dutch Jansen and Janssen, to Afrikaners Uys and Buys. They are Skapti and Skafti in Iceland, Tik and Tak to the Arabs, and Schulze and Schultze to the Germans.

The bowler hats, umbrellas, hobnailed boots and bristling moustaches are by all accounts typical police accoutrements of the 1930s, grafted on to caricatures of Hergé's father and uncle. The truth of this can be checked by reference to the cover of *Le Miroir*, a Parisian weekly, from 2 March 1919. Two identical bowler-hatted, moustachioed detectives are shown, dead ringers for Thompson and Thomson. One is handcuffed to an anarchist who has just been arrested for attempting to assassinate Monsieur Clemenceau. The other, naturally, holds two umbrellas. Hergé claimed never to have seen the magazine in his life.

Unlike the two men in the photograph, telling the real (cartoon) detectives apart is easy. Thompson's moustache curls inward, Thomson's twirls outward. Usually it is Thompson who says 'to be precise'. From their very first hopeless foray into national dress on page 5 of *Cigars Of The Pharaoh*,[2] their penchant for self-inflicted nasal injury and trail of destroyed hats made them an integral part of the Tintin series. It is typical of them that they should rescue Tintin from a tight corner purely in order to arrest him again. In later years, as Hergé's characterisation became more subtle, he came to feel slightly limited by the twins' simple idiocy, and left them out of *Tintin In Tibet* and *Flight 714* altogether; but the 1930s were their heyday, and their antics in *The Black Island* and *Land Of Black Gold* rank with the finest moments of any Tintin adventure.

Besides the Thompsons, *Cigars Of The Pharaoh* yields many other fine comic characters who reappear throughout the series. The bulbous-nosed Rastapopoulos, glimpsed briefly in the previous book, is introduced properly as a benevolent film producer in the D. W. Griffith mould. Later, of course, he becomes Tintin's best known adversary, but we don't discover his true role until the end of the story, in *The Blue Lotus*'s final pages. A friend thought of the name, and it cracked Hergé up. Rastapopoulos' assistant of later years, Captain Allan, an unscrupulous chain-smoking English merchant seaman with an equally daft nose, also makes his debut in *Cigars Of The Pharaoh*. This, however, is cheating on Hergé's part. Allan was never in the original – his real debut came in *The Crab With The Golden*

Claws – and the sequence on pages 9–12 in which he appears was written in when the book was redrawn in 1955. Presumably Hergé's idea was to test the waters, so to speak, prior to pairing off Rastapopoulos and Allan in *The Red Sea Sharks* the following year.

Another interesting villain to pop up in *Cigars Of The Pharaoh* is the gunrunner who rescues Tintin from the storm on page 13, only to be exposed by him five pages later. This seeming ingratitude masks Hergé's own ambivalent attitude to the man he was caricaturing, Henri de Monfreid. Writer-adventurer Monfreid had influenced Hergé, and *Cigars Of The Pharaoh* in particular, through his books *Secrets Of The Red Sea* and *The Hashish Cruise*. Unlike Tintin, though, Monfreid was happy to step outside the law – it was all part of the game. Hergé detested war; the Great War had been played out close enough to his home city for him to understand its realities. Anyone who fuelled war was committing a mortal sin in his eyes, and so he came out against the initially sympathetic Monfreid character in the end.

Altogether more engaging and humorous is Oliveira da Figueira, the Portuguese master salesman with a convincing line in chat, who pops up in all the Middle Eastern books. He manages to sell Tintin a top hat, a pair of skis, a watering can, a parrot, a bow tie, a golf club, an alarm clock, a pair of braces, a pail and a kennel, and becomes a friend for life in the process. Then there is Sophocles Sarcophagus, the first of Hergé's numerous experiments with potty professors, that culminate with the creation of Cuthbert Calculus. Sarcophagus already exhibits some of his successor's more pronounced traits: absent-mindedness, Edwardian dress and an unusual beard.

The credit for this sudden deluge of first-rate characters must, of course, go to Hergé in the first instance. Yet it is obvious that his thinking had been radically diverted from its former tack since the end of *Tintin In America*. In fact, the vital spark had almost certainly been provided by a friend of Hergé's brother, Paul Jamin. Hergé had struck up an immediate friendship with 'Jam', as he was called, which had been cemented on the discovery that Jam was a humorist and caricaturist. On the spur of the moment, Hergé decided to take Jam on as a collaborator at the *Petit Vingtième*, working with him from *Cigars Of The Pharaoh* onwards. The young man was the sort to find humour in everything, especially in Hergé's marriage and in Adolf Hitler, attacks on whom soon began to appear in the *Vingtième*. Either the Abbé was beginning to have second thoughts, or Hergé was now polarising power away from him successfully.

Jam was an avid reader of the London 'funnies' such as *The Humorist* and *Punch*. It is difficult to imagine the inter-war *Punch* inspiring anyone to such heights; but it did, apparently, give rise to the new direction Paul Jamin took Hergé in. Of course, Hergé was to take on many other collaborators throughout his career, and Jam soon faded out of the picture. All of them stressed that artistic control of Tintin and his fellow characters never once passed out of Hergé's hands. Yet all of them influenced the direction of Tintin in their way, and that direction certainly took one of its most abrupt changes in 1932.

Not only the style of comedy, but the style of adventure too. Whereas *Soviets, Congo* and *America* simply introduced random hazards at intervals, *Cigars Of The Pharaoh*'s mystery plot induces a genuine sense of fear without recourse to a *deus ex machina*. There were a few left-over 'quick thrill' episodes, involving a bat, crocodiles, and two snake scenes, but these were ruthlessly pared away when the book was redrawn. The atmosphere is made more unsettling still by the first of Hergé's celebrated dream sequences: Rastapopoulos and Snowy, in Egyptian dress, carry Tintin off, while Sarcophagus rocks the baby Tintin in a crib and smokes one of the Pharaoh's cigars. Tintinologists have long tried to find the hidden meaning in these dreams, but if anyone was dreaming then it wasn't Hergé. He merely used the illogic of dreams for comic effect. When Captain Haddock sat naked in an audience of parrots in *The Castafiore Emerald*, for instance, Hergé was not interested in any subliminal meaning, only that he found the idea funny.

In *Cigars Of The Pharaoh*, however, the dream, the Rajaijah poison of madness and the mummified archaeologists are all used to construct an air of menace absent from the previous stories. A school lecture about Tutankhamun, by an archaeologist old boy named Jean Capart, seems to have been the long-term inspiration for the story. The opening of the tomb by Howard Carter's expedition in 1922 and the curse that afflicted the explorers involved had long fascinated Hergé. On this occasion, though, he saved the curse for *The Seven Crystal Balls*, keeping the tomb and using it as the headquarters of a gang of drug smugglers transporting opium in hollowed-out cigars.

Despite his use of one central set of villains for the first time, the plot of *Cigars Of The Pharaoh* still obviously suffers from being written on a week-by-week basis, with not enough forward planning. Hergé even instituted a mystery column in the *Petit Vingtième*, which ran as far as *King Ottokar's Sceptre*, in which readers were asked to give their solution to the quandaries Hergé had unkindly dumped Tintin in. Whether he ever used any of their plot suggestions is not recorded.

The glaring flaw in the plot is that the story is divided clumsily into two halves, set first in Egypt then in India. Hergé's intention was to set the entire first part of *Tintin In The East* in Egypt – he even called it *The Cairo Affair* at one point during the *Petit Vingtième* version – but he soon ran out of Egyptian ideas and switched the action a few hundred miles to the east. Tintin's arrival in India necessitates a string of absurd coincidences, whereby he bumps into Professor Sarcophagus and the Thompson twins once more, completely by chance, in a subcontinent of several hundred million people. This uncomfortable join does, however, give Hergé the chance to make partial amends for *Tintin In The Congo*, by revealing his villains to be a group of British colonial thoroughbreds[3] in suspiciously Ku-Klux-Klan-like hoods, who are undermining the native administration.

The sudden diversion of *Cigars Of The Pharaoh* to

India caused a headache when the story was packaged up in book form, and a map was inserted into page one suggesting that the whole thing had been planned from the start. It showed a notional route from Port Said via Bombay to Shanghai, similar to the route which Tintin eventually took to the end of *The Blue Lotus*. The modern British version substitutes an altogether different map, showing an aborted Mediterranean cruise. This is more logical, but then the British edition gets into a terrible tangle over the introduction of Rastapopoulos. Because *Cigars* was one of the last books to be translated into English, Tintin's arch enemy was considered too well established in the minds of English-speaking readers to start introducing him for the first time. Hence the following absurd conversation: Rastapopoulos – 'One day you'll regret you crossed my path. Just remember: my name is Rastapopoulos!' Tintin – 'Rastapopoulos? Rastapopoulos? Ah! I've got it: the millionaire film tycoon, King of Cosmos Pictures . . . and it's not the first time we've met . . .'

The first book version of *Cigars* came out in 1934, but when it was shortened, redrawn and coloured in 1955, other oddities were thrown up. When Tintin is taken prisoner on page 15[4] by Sheikh Patrash Pasha[5] he is shown a copy of *Destination Moon*. At the time *Cigars* was being redrawn, *Destination Moon* was the latest story to appear in book form, but its inclusion is not exactly logical. In the *Petit Vingtième* Tintin was shown a copy of *Tintin In America*, which was further changed somewhere along the way into *Tintin In The Congo*.

There were a few other cosmetic cuts made in 1955:

Mr Bearding, a cotton planter with a vast black beard (Hergé found beards immensely funny), disappeared altogether. The Polish-sounding writer Zlotskwtz, who was actually supposed to be Hungarian, became the poet Zloty of no fixed nationality. A scene which would have slotted in on the bottom line of page 57, where the evil Fakir piles explosives against the door behind which Tintin and Co. are locked, was also cut. Snowy had removed the danger by urinating on the fuse, a trick he also pulled off in *The Shooting Star*. Once was enough. The most important changes of 1955, though, were those made for artistic reasons. The 1950s and 1960s were the peak period of Hergé's artistic ability. At the time of the original *Cigars* he was still feeling his way. In particular, much of the grammar of the comic strip which he was to develop himself had not yet been formalised. Pick up any modern Tintin book today, and you will see that Tintin always moves from left to right, advancing the story. Obstacles come at him from right to left, and when he moves in that direction he is usually experiencing a setback. In the original *Cigars Of The Pharaoh* this is not at all the case, and Tintin had to be pointed in the right direction in 1955.

As Hergé prepared to move into the third, Chinese phase of *Tintin In The East*, he had developed a rich comic style and had the essentials of plot structure well within his grasp. These new developments had not escaped the *Petit Vingtième* readership – the parent paper *Le Vingtième Siècle* was now selling ten times more copies than normal on Tintin day. Still missing, though, were the artistic skills and meticulous authenticity that characterise a Tintin story. A startling development was to occur during the first few pages of the future *Blue Lotus*, which not only heralded the arrival of these, but which permanently and profoundly affected Hergé's entire life.

8

The Blue Lotus

Le Lotus Bleu

The great event had small beginnings. It all started with a letter. Hergé had decided to announce in the *Petit Vingtième* that it would not be long before Tintin visited China. The Chinese interested him: Belgium was home to a great many Chinese Catholics, just as China was home to a number of Belgian missionaries busily attempting to convert the Chinese. Hergé already had a few Chinese friends, including Père Lou, a politician who had abandoned his job in Shanghai to become a monk at Loppen. Hergé's knowledge of the country itself, though, was as sketchy as his knowledge of Russia, the Congo, or anywhere else that Tintin had been. On page 67 of *Soviets*, for instance, two Chinese had been depicted as unscrupulous pigtailed torturers straight out of the Middle Ages, the type who crumple at the slightest sign of fisticuffs. In short, typical yellow foreigners.

This is where Chang came in. Anxious to avoid a repetition of this racial stereotyping, the Abbé Gosset, who was chaplain to a group of Chinese Catholic students at Louvain University, wrote to Hergé and implored him to 'do a little research'. Hergé took up the challenge, and through Gosset, was introduced to a young student at the Brussels Palace of Fine Arts. His name was Chang Chon-Ren, and as far as Hergé was concerned, he opened a window on the whole world.

First, he taught Hergé Chinese calligraphy and painting techniques, how to use perspective, and the importance of a clear line. Prior to this, Hergé had regarded drawing Tintin as a 'game' or a 'joke'. Now he took it seriously. So good were the drawings in *The Blue Lotus* that the current version contains the earliest original artwork still used in modern editions, although the book was trimmed down and coloured in 1946, and most of the backgrounds were embellished. The first four pages, which generically belong to *The Cigars Of The Pharaoh*, were redrawn completely in 1946, and the change between these newer pages and the rest of the book is quite clear. As well as in the drawings, Chang's graphic influence can be seen in the special Tintin typeface, which now decorates the covers of all Hergé's books.

Chang also impressed upon Hergé the need for authenticity, so that for the first time with *The Blue Lotus*, every location is scrupulously accurate, every fact verifiable. For *Cigars Of The Pharaoh* he had merely nipped down to the local museum, the same place where he had found Aniota, the leopard-man of *Tintin In The Congo*; but now, streets, buildings and landscapes would be exactly as in real life. Many of the pictures, such as the collapsed railway track on page 42,[1] came from photographs of real events taking place at the

76

time, either from photo-news magazines or from the *Vingtième's* own photographic department, where Hergé used to work. Hergé was beginning to learn the value of photographic accuracy as an aesthetic attraction, heightening the comic contrast with those faces and figures he did wish to caricature.

With this new authentic approach came a radical political perspective on the events taking place in the Far East. Chang told Hergé the true story of the Japanese invasion of China, a war that was still going on; how the provocative blowing up of the Moukden railwayline, allegedly carried out by Chinese bandits, had been stage-managed by the Japanese; how the Japanese were presiding over atrocities in China that did not appear in the largely sympathetic western press; and how the authorities in the International Settlement in Shanghai turned a blind eye to these Japanese activities. Hergé inserted all of it, verbatim, into *The Blue Lotus*. Tintin found himself cast in the role of international social crusader and chronicler of major world events, a role that was only interrupted by the arrival of the Second World War. In the process of this education, Hergé also found in Chang a firm and lasting friend, possibly for the first time in his life.

Looking back after Hergé's death, Chang said: 'We were like two brothers. I suggested to him that to use real events as the inspiration for his adventures would be a better idea . . . the oeuvre would have a historical value, divested of pure fantasy and artificial sentiments. Thus *The Blue Lotus* was born. At that time I visited Hergé once a week. We spoke of history, anecdote, costumes, poetry, art, the countryside and so on. As soon as the drawings were inked in, I drew the Chinese characters in different handwriting.'[2] Hergé and Chang worked on the text together, and Chang's signature can still be seen in two places. It is on the front of a warehouse at the docks, at the bottom right-hand corner of page 55;[3] and, in the delightful crowd scene on page 45,[4] where the Thompsons turn up in Hukow dressed 'inconspicuously' as Mandarins, Chang's signature can be seen on the green and red sign at the back next to the blue striped awning.

The Thompson twins are not the only characters in the book who represent Hergé's former ignorance of things Chinese. Hergé directly attacks his own pre-Chang assumptions through the mouth of Tintin: 'Lots of Europeans still believe that all Chinese are cunning and cruel and wear pigtails, are always inventing tortures, and eating rotten eggs and swallows' nests. The same stupid Europeans are quite convinced that all Chinese girls suffer agonies with bandages designed to prevent their feet developing normally. They're even convinced that Chinese rivers are full of unwanted babies, thrown in when they are born.' In return for disabusing him of these notions, Hergé made Chang into a character in the book, the first real friend that his alter ego Tintin ever had. Chang's surname was changed slightly: Chon-Ren became Chong-Chen, an adjustment which has confused almost every writer on the subject into thinking that Chong-Chen was his real name.

Trouble was looming, however, over the story's radical political stance. The attack on the Japanese was vitriolic. Hergé portrayed them all as ugly, unscrupulous, militaristic men with short legs and rectangular teeth. Chang's Chinese posters shouted slogans such as 'Down with Japanese goods!' and 'Down with imperialism!' from almost every frame. The attack on the 'imperialists', the British and Americans who ran the Shanghai settlement, is if anything even stronger than the attack on the Japanese. Gibbons, the American steel trader, is portrayed as a greasy, loud-mouthed, overweight, racist bigot. Dawson, the slimy and corrupt British Chief of Police, is used to criticise the compromises inherent in the settlement, and is directly accused of complicity with the Japanese. Tokyo's resignation from the League of Nations, a real event which had taken place in 1933, is exposed as a piece of barefaced hypocrisy. Hergé's political thinking had turned full circle inside four years – if indeed he could previously be said to have had any political thoughts. Those who have never forgiven Hergé for *Tintin In The Congo* still seek to accuse him of racism towards the Japanese over *The Blue Lotus*, but this accusation stupidly misses the point of the story.

The Japanese were furious. The Japanese ambassador protested vehemently to the Belgian government, threatening to take them to the International Court of Justice at The Hague, and demanding that the story be banned. Japanese-Belgian relations tottered. The Belgian military became involved, protesting that the subject was not fit for Belgian children. Hergé admitted for the first time that he was not solely drawing for children any more. Belgian children, none the less, lapped it up. The

Chinese found they suddenly had a voice in the west, albeit an unusual one, defending them against the aggressors who had invaded their country. When the dust had settled, Madame Chiang Kai-Shek, the wife of the President, formally invited Hergé to China. The gathering turmoil of war in the east and then in Europe prevented him taking up the invitation, but did, ultimately, prove *The Blue Lotus* right and the western press wrong. What with one thing and another, it was not until 1973 that Hergé finally got round to visiting Madame Chiang Kai-Shek in her Taiwanese exile.

Developments in China and the onset of war also parted Hergé from Chang, when his friend had to return to Shanghai. The seeds of interest in Taoism,[5] mysticism and Chinese culture which Chang had implanted gradually flowered, and as the years went by Hergé began to miss Chang with what amounted to an ache. Although Tintin had found new friends, Hergé seemed unable to fill the hole in his life. In the 1950s the need to find his lost friend once more spilled over into his work, in *Tintin In Tibet*.

Many a Tintin story begins and ends in the mundane setting of home, and this one is no exception. After buttonholing Chinese people all over the world, in Taiwan especially, Hergé finally struck lucky in his home suburb of Etterbeek. Towards the end of 1975, he was introduced to a Mr Wei, who had lived in Etterbeek all his life; Wei's wife recognised Chang Chon-Ren as her husband's godfather, the director of a sculpture academy in Shanghai. Infuriatingly, Chang turned out to be living in the same house as he had done in 1934

– Hergé had never bothered to check. Shades of *Red Rackham's Treasure* indeed!

After Hergé's death, the long-lost original manuscript of *The Blue Lotus* was found at the Studios Hergé and put on display in Tintin's sixtieth birthday exhibition. Looking at it now, Tintin hasn't quite found his settled shape yet – he's still a round-faced, slightly hunched little chap, compared to his final incarnation of *King Ottokar's Sceptre* onwards. The Thompsons and Snowy, too, were to be marginally redesigned. For 1934, though, it's a marvellous piece of comic strip art. The foundations of the modern Tintin style, painstaking accuracy combined with sparing caricature, have clearly been laid. Many adult Tintin fans regard it as their favourite story, perhaps because it was so ground-breaking. Certainly it is not often that a children's comic disturbs the waters of international diplomacy.

Of course it has proved impossible to modernise the story, and it rather stands out amid the timelessness of the other Tintin books. The International Settlement in Shanghai is, in retrospect, one of the more obscure settings a Tintin adventure could have, perhaps because the western media gave the place so little coverage. *The Blue Lotus* was one of the very last Tintin stories to be translated into English, in 1983, precisely because of this apparently insurmountable hurdle. Hergé had already replotted much of the *Land Of Black Gold* at the insistence of the British publishers (as well as modernising *The Black Island*:) it too made dated political points in dated settings and incidentally was terribly unkind to the British abroad. We should be grateful that attitudes had changed sufficiently by the 1980s to allow *The Blue Lotus* to be published with its historical virginity intact. 'We learned that our audience was a great deal more receptive and sophisticated than we had realised,' says Michael Turner.

The lessons that Hergé himself learned from Chang and *The Blue Lotus* merged with the lessons he had learned from *The Cigars Of The Pharaoh* to create the modern Tintin. It was of course some years before all the ingredients were to coalesce perfectly, and there were many new characters, and new artistic techniques to come. The rich vein of well-researched political satire in *The Blue Lotus* did, however, point the way forward for the immediate future. It had taken a lot of courage to stick at the story in the face of such criticism, as a result of which Hergé decided it was time for another change. He would continue to attack the manipulative, the aggressive and the power-hungry of this world, at Chang's instigation, but not directly by name; henceforth he would satirise them through parody instead. In the process, he was to create an entire world geography of his own.

9

The Broken Ear

L'Oreille Cassée

By the 1970s, it was possible for Tintin to board a plane in Sondonesia (not a million miles from Indonesia) and fly to Khemed, a desert nation midway between Saudi Arabia and the Lebanon, which was curiously reminiscent of Jordan. Or he could visit the Bordurian capital Szohôd, a mercilessly accurate parody of a pre-glasnost East European city, right down to the many representations of the dictator Marshal Kûrvi-Tasch, a figure with an uncanny resemblance to Stalin. Or perhaps Klow, the mineral water capital of the world, in a guardedly friendly but authoritarian Syldavia, whose mosques, hills and coastline look for all the world like Yugoslavia's.

Before all these, Hergé had laid the foundations of his world with two South American dictatorships – San Theodoros and Nuevo Rico in *The Broken Ear*. Each was a fully-fledged 1930s banana republic, with bandidos in sombreros, head-shrinking natives and a change of government almost hourly. This type of setting is now so hackneyed, it is easy to forget that it was not quite so unoriginal back in 1935. These were not just any old banana republics. San Theodoros and Nuevo Rico were direct parodies of Bolivia and Paraguay, while the story itself constituted a fierce attack on the international arms dealers who were fuelling their long-running feud.

The 'War of the Gran Chaco' between the two countries, which had ground on senselessly for four years at a cost of 100,000 lives, was another great undiscovered war – virtually unknown in the west[1]. Yet it was the west which had originated and now controlled the conflict. Two big oil companies, both seeking the exclusive concession to a disputed border area, had encouraged the two countries to attack each other. On top of that, the soldiers of both sides were being killed with weapons supplied by the same man: Sir Basil Zaharoff, a Greek arms dealer who had been knighted by Britain after making his fortune selling British weapons to all sides during the First World War.

There was something obscene about the sleek Zaharoff lining his pockets at the expense of thousands of soldiers' lives, so Hergé inserted the facts wholesale – just as he had done with the Sino-Japanese war – into the *Petit Vingtième*. This was real education for the Abbé's little charges! The vitriolic attack is principally carried by the scene on pages 31–5.[2] Parody it may have been, but the disguise was a thin one. The war of the Gran Chaco became the war of the Gran Chapo, with both sides obtaining their arms from Sir Basil Mazaroff of the Vicking Arms Company Limited, an outfit sounding suspiciously like Vickers. The English translators tactfully abandoned the British connection and offered instead a German called Bazarov.

The satire of *The Broken Ear* is less overt than that in *The Blue Lotus*, not because of the partial concealment provided by the fictional setting, but because it is buried much further down in an ostensibly straightforward mystery plot. After the furore over *The Blue Lotus*, the first half of *The Broken Ear* deliberately gives little hint of what is to follow. This thriller device, although borrowed heavily from *The Maltese Falcon*, is actually rather good. Certainly it is Hergé's most complex plot yet, by a long way.

A broken-eared statuette is stolen from a Brussels museum, because, it transpires, there is a priceless diamond inside. Tintin goes after it, but there are two desperadoes on the thief's trail too. The plot is littered with various fake statuettes, and there is a talking parrot with a clue in its head. As the action moves to San Theodoros, the second half of the story is played out against the background of the Gran Chapo war.

Despite all these enticing ingredients, however, there is something disappointing overall about *The Broken Ear*. This is partly because the book's various elements don't gel together well. The satirical thrust does not emerge through the main plot as in *The Blue Lotus*, but beside it. Especially out of place is a laboured sequence set in the jungle homeland of the Arumbaya tribe, which appears to have been drawn in a hurry.

Hergé had begun *The Broken Ear* in a great flurry of meticulous, Chang-inspired research, as he put it, 'out of a sense of honesty to my readers'. The museum scene at the beginning is scrupulously correct in every detail, right down to the statuette itself. This was a genuine artefact, discovered in a real Brussels museum by Hergé; a pre-Colombian fetish from Peru, some 55 centimetres high, with a worn (rather than chipped) right ear. Zaharoff, too, is caricatured in every detail. Yet despite some commentators' pretentious comparisons with Giorgio de Chirico, Hergé's South America does not have the same ring of truth as Hergé's China. The raw material was there – the cover picture of Tintin in a dugout canoe, for example, was taken straight from a news photo – but as the book goes on, one can sense the enthusiasm for meticulous detail draining away.

By 1935 he was putting in an awful lot of work on the *Petit Vingtième*, including a full-colour cover illustration every week, together with various outside commercial commissions. Tintin's carefully drawn backgrounds were taking up too much of his time. He was getting sloppier. Vegetation (a Hergé speciality) was either wrong – bananas growing downwards instead of upwards – or not there at all. The deterioration in the artistic quality of the jungle between pages 46 and 52[3] is remarkable: over six pages, the amount of background detail steadily decreases to zero.

Nor is the language well researched. On *The Blue Lotus* he had enjoyed the advantage of collaborating with a fluent Chinese speaker: on *The Broken Ear*, not surprisingly, he knew nobody who could speak any South American Indian dialects. Although he had the linguistic content of future Tintin books checked over by local language students, he had no choice on *The*

Broken Ear but to invent. The result – a rendering of his own language into apparent pidgin Indian – is mildly amusing but ultimately a little tiresome.

Another possible reason for *The Broken Ear*'s slightly lacklustre quality is the colouring. *The Blue Lotus* was coloured with a flourish in 1946. *The Broken Ear* had figured among Hergé's first ever attempts at shortening and colouring existing artwork, in 1943. The colours, mostly a series of pale washes, are a touch lifeless, and betray the story's black-and-white origins. After re-colouring a short-lived version of *The Black Island* as well, Hergé took on the professional colourist E. P. Jacobs as his colleague in 1944, and learned a great deal from him before their ways eventually parted.

If *The Broken Ear* was not entirely successful, Hergé did manage to salvage several ideas from it for later use. The man-eating parrot (page 12) turned up in *The Castafiore Emerald*. The last-minute reprieve from the firing squad (page 21) reappeared in *Tintin And The Picaros*. The fireball (page 27) and a dream sequence which only appeared in the *Petit Vingtième*,[4] where a native climbs through Tintin's window, were re-used in *The Seven Crystal Balls*. The car crash in the ravine (page 40) made another appearance in *The Calculus Affair*, and Snowy's escape from being washed away (page 44) showed up in *The Shooting Star*.

One or two of the characters were to stand the test of time as well, although the stock was not so rich this time as in *Tintin In The East*. In 1975, *Tintin And The Picaros* included the return of Doctor Ridgewell, as well as Pablo, who in the *Petit Vingtième* had been known as

'Juan Paolino, the terror of Las Dopicos'. Then there is the absent-minded professor who goes for a stroll on page 6, only to become tremendously confused by the parrot. He undoubtedly contributed something to the development of Cuthbert Calculus. The longest-serving of the *Broken Ear* characters though, is the mercurial General Alcazar. Here we meet him as a gloriously extrovert comic-book dictator, engaged in one constant battle with General Tapioca, for possession of the Presidential Palace in Las Dopicos, and in another with General Mogador, occupant of the Presidential Palace in Sanfacion. Alcazar creates Colonels at such a rate that he has 3487 of them, to 49 corporals. In *Tintin And The Picaros*, we find the volatile General back playing South American power politics again; but in the interim, he turns up in *The Seven Crystal Balls* and *The Red Sea Sharks*, cutting a rather sinister figure in exile.

The Broken Ear was also the first Tintin adventure to deal with the hunt for an object, and the first to start and finish in home surroundings. Tintin had come a long way since the start of *Tintin In The East*, when he had been a globetrotting reporter in search of quick thrills. Now a series of Tintin adventures were to be mystery stories following the *Broken Ear* pattern.

The only thing Hergé deliberately did not repeat was his brief experiment in meting out sticky ends to his villains. In a bizarre finale to *The Broken Ear*, Ramon and Alonzo drown and are carried off to a tasteless pink hell by little black devils. Two other characters die in the story, the sculptor Balthazar, offstage, and Colonel Diaz, who gets blown to smithereens by his own bomb (the circular black variety, of course). A few years later and poor Diaz would have ended up behind bars in far more wholesome a fashion.

The strong moral (and perhaps more importantly) political lessons of *The Broken Ear* did not meet with universal approval from the guardians of French and Belgian youth. The editor of *Coeurs Vaillants* magazine professed himself disturbed by Tintin's independent attitude. Four deaths and the besmirching of a fine, upstanding arms dealer's reputation didn't help. He commissioned a new strip for younger readers, which was to feature a Tintinesque hero in a family setting, with a mother, a father, a sister, a pet and definitely no obscure Third World conflicts. Jo, Zette and Jocko came into being as a result, in 1936. Hergé took Jo and Zette from a brother and sister he had used in a promotional strip for Antoine the confectioner's, two years previously. Jocko the monkey was a toy he'd drawn at home, also as an advertising commission. Jo, Zette, Jocko and Mr and Mrs Legrand got through five innocent adventures, before Hergé became fed up with crowbarring the entire family into every plot development, and gave the lot of them the push. Of course, they never supplanted Tintin.

The Broken Ear had a fascinating sequel, which occurred in 1979 at the Palace of Fine Arts in Brussels. At the time the museum was housing a fiftieth anniversary exhibition of genuine artefacts used by Hergé in the Tintin stories, in which the broken-eared fetish was the star of the show. In a carbon copy of the crime in the book, a thief broke in and stole it from its display.

A letter was sent to the newspaper *Le Soir*, worded similarly to that on page 3 of the book (and also signed 'X'), telling Hergé that the fetish would be returned if he waited by the scene of the crime at a given time with a copy of *The Broken Ear* under his right arm.

Unknown to the villain, though, what he had actually stolen was a fake, placed in the display for just such an eventuality – just as the two villains in the book had also stolen a fake. Ever the humorist, Hergé turned up at the appointed time with a copy of the book under his *left* arm. Clearly this new twist in the plot proved too much for the thief, who never showed. The fake fetish is presumably in his – or her – possession to this day.

The Black Island

L'Ile Noire

In 1937, the next target of Hergé's political satire presented itself clearly, as it would have done for any young satirist with a burning sense of global injustice. No more obscure conflicts – Hergé was thinking big. He would caricature the Nazis themselves, through the eyes of one of their victims, the imaginary nation of Syldavia. His head whirled with ideas. Perhaps a London conference on the future of Syldavia, with the little monarchy being sold down the river by larger nations? Perhaps the death of the Syldavian King, leaving only a nephew with an uncertain claim to the throne? Perhaps a valuable mineral discovery on Syldavian territory would provide the excuse? Or perhaps he should use a metaphorical device, in the shape of a mysterious meteor plunging to earth there?

Then strangely, all these lofty plans were put in abeyance by dreams. Dreams of white, the frozen north, a car stuck in a snowdrift. Hergé's dreams were often vivid and obviously important to him as an inspiration, but these white dreams are disturbingly reminiscent of the terrifying and recurring nightmares that followed the virtual collapse of his personal life in the 1950s. The comparison is not an idle one. This was not an especially happy time for Hergé. He had made the radical decision to leave the offices of the *Vingtième* and work from home as a freelance, giving him more time to concentrate on the quality of the Tintin stories. His work undoubtedly improved, but as so often in later years, improved working practices brought with them a concomitant unhappiness. Hergé was lonely, and missed Jam and the other friends who inhabited the carefree *Vingtième* offices. He was working without a collaborator again, and would do so for another three years.

Tintin's northern digression became *The Black Island*. Despite abortive plans for the boy reporter to tour Greenland or the Klondike, in the end he got no further than the west coast of Scotland. The car in the snowdrift was relegated to the cover of a wartime greetings card. He saved the metaphorical meteor up for *The Shooting Star*. The anti-German message of the postponed Syldavian adventure was reflected only in the nationality of the chief villain, the newly invented Dr Müller, described by Hergé as a Rastapopoulos figure prepared to risk his own life. Instead, *The Black Island* took on an identity of its own, influenced by current events.

The story concerned a gang of forgers, a topical crime in the 1930s. It was the first out-and-out Tintin crime story since *Cigars Of The Pharaoh* and the last until the war. The forgers operated out of Craig Dhui castle in the Western Isles, protected by local fear of the legendary 'Beast of Kiltoch' (actually a rather amiable gorilla called Ranko). The beast was an obvious amalgam of

King Kong (hugely popular in the 1930s) and the Loch Ness Monster, which had allegedly been sighted by over fifty people on a single occasion in October of the previous year. The television set on which Tintin watches the Thompson twins' involuntary aerial display was another reflection of the times, and one peculiar to Britain. BBC-TV had started their experimental transmissions in 1936. Where the modern Tintin rushes into a room with a gun to exclaim 'It's only a television set!', in the original *Petit Vingtième* version he rushes in to exclaim excitedly, 'It's a television set!'[1]

The Black Island also reveals a convenient, hitherto unsuspected regard for Britain and the British. In the light of events on the mainland of Europe, Britain in 1937 must have presented a more tranquil and appealing aspect than before. Hergé's idea of the British Isles was, however, a little quaint. Firemen pulled their fire engines by hand, policemen rushed around the countryside brandishing guns, and adverts said things like 'Drink a gin and lime and be happy'. At the turn of the 1960s, when the time came to consider an English translation, Methuen were concerned by these inaccuracies. They urged Hergé to embark upon a modernised version.

'Hergé was not in a hurry to do that,' says Bob de Moor, Hergé's chief post-war assistant. By the 1960s, Hergé's youthful motivation had been somewhat eroded, especially with *The Castafiore Emerald* in production; but he had the staff to handle the job instead, so Bob de Moor was despatched to Britain in Hergé's place. De Moor set about his task wholeheartedly and meticulously, following Tintin's exact footsteps across

Britain with camera and sketchpad, ultimately to produce a series of background drawings indistinguishable from Hergé originals. Says Michael Turner, 'There was enormous excitement about the redrawing of *The Black Island*; certainly you got a feeling of efficiency, that it would all fit together. I remember when Bob came over, everything was beautifully organised, the machine was really rolling.'

De Moor began with the white cliffs of Dover (page 8), then to Bateman's in Sussex (the model for Dr Müller's house – page 13 onwards), Bishop's Stortford Station (page 30), the village of Castlebay on the Isle of Barra (Kiltoch – page 41) and Lochranza Castle on the Isle of Arran (the Black Island itself – page 43). After that he went to Edinburgh to collect a Scottish policeman's uniform, which apparently differed from its English counterpart in minor detail.[2] Fire engines, boats, trains, even down to the correct hooter noise on a British Railways engine, all were faithfully recorded and fitted in to Hergé's original design. Only the planes were drawn separately, by aviation expert Roger Leloup. Unfortunately, though, the advertisement on page 36 still says 'Drink a gin and lime and be happy'. Perhaps De Moor's English was a little on the tentative side.

Although Hergé drew only the characters in the final version, the result, published here in 1966, is a fine piece of work and one of the most beautifully drawn Tintin books. The excellence of *The Black Island* is due also to a strong, cohesive plot which demonstrates the rapid strides Hergé was making in that department by 1937. He had learned the value of visual ideas that kept text to a minimum, attractive settings to show off the action, and unexpected plot twists to keep the reader guessing. The nature of the crime itself is not revealed until page 27,[3] a delay which disturbed Hergé, but he need not have worried. If there is a plot weakness, it lies in the unexpected coincidence which enables Tintin to bump into Müller in the White Hart pub after the German has given him the slip on the train. On page 5,[4] too, there is an echo of early, slapstick days. Being chased by the Thompson twins (still convinced he is up to no good, four adventures on), Tintin produces a false beard and hat from nowhere. It is a direct steal from the equally silly scene on page 48 of *Cigars Of The Pharaoh*, where it should have been left. These isolated incidents represent the last flicker of 1920s Tintin.

Curiously, the modernised *Black Island* was produced by a process divorced from the normal Tintin production method. A glance at any pre-war or wartime Tintin story where the original artwork survives will show a fine drawing line in use. This is not for any other reason than that the original *Petit Vingtième* format was larger, and so the drawings had to be reduced slightly to fit into the modern colour book form. After the war, when Hergé started every story in the colour format, he actually drew his originals double-sized — bigger still — so that the finished version could encapsulate more detail. However, he used a double thickness of line, so that upon reduction the drawings would look happy at normal size. *The Black Island* differs in that to celebrate the new version, it was drawn at the old *Vingtième* size, but using the new thicker line. A special limited

Vingtième-size edition was then released, before the drawings were reduced to normal. The result is that *The Black Island* has a slightly richer look than usual. If any fine detail is missing, such is Bob de Moor's skill that you wouldn't notice.

As a comedy, as well as artistically, *The Black Island* outstrips its predecessors. As with all late 1930s Tintin stories, the main comic thrust is provided by the Thompson twins. Their exploits when handcuffed together by Tintin at the start are memorable, but their air display towards the end of the story – when they magisterially commandeer a plane only to discover that the man at the controls is a mechanic who has never flown before – is quite superb. Hergé also enlarges upon the comic potential of drunkenness, touched upon in *The Broken Ear*, by giving Snowy a taste for Loch Lomond whisky. Snowy's ability to overdose at the most inconvenient moments was later applied more fruitfully to Captain Haddock, of course. Hergé did get one British detail right in 1937: in the original version, Snowy's favourite tipple was not Loch Lomond, but a wee dram of Johnnie Walker.[5]

Whatever its unusual origins, *The Black Island* was ultimately a triumph, and one of the most popular Tintin stories; but it was also, in a sense, a digression from the business at hand. With his next story, the delayed Syldavian drama, Hergé was about to enter the most dangerous phase of his professional life.

11

King Ottokar's Sceptre

Le Sceptre d'Ottokar

The biting political satire of *King Ottokar's Sceptre*, or *Tintin In Syldavia* as it was known in the *Petit Vingtième*, put Hergé firmly back on the crusading course that Chang had mapped out for him; but whereas earlier in the decade he had helped to pioneer European opposition to the expansion of the far right, now he was just one of many plaintive voices. *King Ottokar's Sceptre* is no less powerful for that. Viewed from the first few frames of the story, in August 1938 – another low-key domestic opening, with Tintin finding a mislaid brief-case on a park bench – the only possible destination Hergé could have envisaged for himself was the inside of a Nazi prison cell. Those who questioned his allegiance and his bravery after the war would have done well to remember just how courageous a book *King Ottokar's Sceptre* was for him to be writing by the story's close in August 1939.

The plot was directly inspired by the 'Anschluss', Hitler's annexation of Austria, which had taken place in March 1938; but in the ingenious Balkan creations of Syldavia and Borduria Hergé manages to encompass not

only Germany and Austria, but a good handful of
nations under threat from Nazism. King Muskar XIII of
Syldavia is the target of the Iron Guard, a fifth column
who plan to steal the ceremonial sceptre of Ottokar
without which he is not permitted to rule. Thereafter,
under the command of Müsstler, the Iron Guard leader,
Bordurian forces plan to seize control of the Syldavian
capital Klow, ostensibly in defence of Bordurian nation-
als – who will be beaten up on the day to provide a
suitable excuse.

The name Müsstler is, of course, a straightforward
combination of Hitler and Mussolini, he of the Abbé's
desk *circa* 1925. The other parallels are less well known.
The Iron Guard, for instance, was a real organisation
threatening the throne of King Carol II of Rumania.
The whole question of the Syldavian succession referred
to Belgium, Hergé's own ill-defended base, and Léopold
III's succession as King to Albert I. The name Ottokar
(deriving from the medieval Kings of Bohemia), and the
Bohemian architecture of Kropow Castle in particular,
conjured up Czechoslovakia, Hitler's annexation of the
Sudetenland, and his eventual occupation of the whole
of that country. The mosques of the Syldavian countryside and the dress of its peasants paralleled the Kingdom
of Yugoslavia, then under direct threat from Italy.

Borduria itself was Germany. Its officers wore SS-
style uniforms, and when Tintin stole a Bordurian plane
in the original magazine version, it rather unsubtly had
'Heinkel' written on it. The contrast between Borduria's
muscular Fascism and the quiet rural idyll it threatened
was pointed, even poignant. Of course Syldavia was an

idealised portrayal of central Europe between the wars – a benevolent monarchy, peaceful village life, sturdy peasants puffing on large pipes – but once again, those who criticise Hergé for showing royalist leanings have completely missed the point. *King Ottokar's Sceptre* was meant to be a polemical statement, not a travelogue.

Of the three best pre-war Tintin books, *King Ottokar's Sceptre* probably has the edge over *The Blue Lotus* and *The Black Island*. There is barely a spare frame in its tightly constructed plot – a classic locked room mystery, in which something apparently impossible happens within a sealed place and no one works out how it is done until the end.[1] The satire emerges through the mystery, not beside it (as in *The Broken Ear*), or even partially as a background device (as in *The Blue Lotus*). Admittedly, Hergé had the advantage of postulating a sequence of imaginary events, rather than having to follow real ones as in the invasion of Manchuria, but the sheer vitality of the Syldavian setting is captivating.

Hergé obviously enjoyed giving his imagination free rein on Syldavia. The centre of the book is taken up by a three-page brochure outlining the geography and history of the country. The accuracy of this was unexpectedly confirmed in 1976, during an archaeological dig at Prague's St Vitus Cathedral. Astonishingly the diggers turned up a real sceptre, hitherto unknown, which had belonged to a real King Ottokar who ruled the area from 1253 to 1273.

The lush appearance of the ceremonial costumes at the Syldavian court is the responsibility of Hergé's colourist E. P. Jacobs, who redesigned them when the book was coloured in 1947. Previously, Hergé had based the castle ceremonial upon the jubilee of George V of England, and the uniforms upon the Beefeaters at the Tower of London, but Jacobs undertook the mammoth task of Balkanising them all. For the most part, however, *King Ottokar's Sceptre* was originally drawn as you see it now. Satisfyingly, Tintin is finally starting to look like Tintin.

The Thompsons, too, are finding their feet. For the first time in five adventures, they stop wanting to arrest Tintin and become firm friends. They are on top form here, falling off motorbikes, slipping head over heels on polished floors, blowing up Tintin's flat, and generally doing far more damage as friends than they ever did as enemies. Of the other characters, the Alembick brothers take their place as the latest in Hergé's long line of professors with remarkable beards (roll on Calculus!). Hector Alembick, the nice one, was called Nestor Alembique in the original magazine version, a name that had to be changed after the arrival of Nestor the butler in *The Secret Of The Unicorn*. Then there is Colonel Boris Jorgen, of minor significance, not clearly identified here by name but later to perish in space in *Explorers On The Moon*.

Towering over all of these, although her debut here is restricted to a cameo role, is of course Bianca Castafiore – the 'Milanese Nightingale', the vast soprano whose glass-shattering performances of the Jewel Song from *Faust* follow Tintin unerringly round the world, and who later causes Captain Haddock so much grief. La Castafiore, like Jolyon Wagg, held a special place in

Hergé's life. Opera and insurance salesmen were his two pet dislikes, and in later years, when he was starting to draw his own frustrations out through Haddock, he often wilfully tortured himself with unexpected visits from one or other of these two. Or, on a particularly bad day, both.

'Opera bores me, to my great shame,' he confessed. 'What's more, it makes me laugh.' He found it impossible to take seriously a chorus of men in false beards chanting 'We must go! we must go!' over and over again without actually moving a muscle. In every soprano he saw only a vast fat woman (not surprising, as many of them are) with the ear-splitting voice of his Aunt Ninie. As Castafiore got older, though, her personality grew further away from Hergé's aunt's and closer to that of Maria Callas. Ever indestructible, she rampaged serenely through Marlinspike crushing everything in her path, getting Haddock's name wrong and treating Nestor like a butcher's boy.

The fact that Castafiore is the only regular female character in the Tintin stories (apart from Tintin's pre-war landlady, the long-suffering Mrs Finch) does not open as many doors on to Hergé's psyche as some would like to think. Any sexual repression inherent in the single-sex nature of Tintin belongs to Belgian morality between the wars, not to Hergé, who was something of a ladies' man. He was, after all, the only kid at St Boniface's Catholic College with a secret large-breasted girlfriend. Naming Tintin's dog after her seems to indicate a sense of mischief more than anything else.

Throughout his life, even if it might be said that his conduct towards his first wife left something to be desired, Hergé tended to put women on a pedestal. They were not a fit subject for ridicule – that would be ungallant; and after all, everybody in the Tintin books, even Tintin himself, is subject to ridicule at some point. Castafiore's inclusion is allowed because she is less a woman than a Sherman tank. She is the exception to the rule. She is never ridiculed. She ridicules.

It is worth making a comparison here with Frank Richards, the celebrated author of the Billy Bunter stories. Although far more prolific than Hergé in an equally long career, Richards too drew neutral heroes, like Tintin extremely brave and honourable, but essentially little more than hero costumes for the reader's imagination to don. His heroes too were surrounded by amiable buffoons who took most of the comic knocks, authority figures to sidestep, villains to defeat, and scarcely any girls. Like Hergé he had an unsettled private life which drifted further, year by year, from his own heroic youthful ideals; like Hergé he was himself childless; and like Hergé he treated women with courtesy, affection and respect, not as fair game for schoolchildren to laugh at in a comic strip.

Although Hergé's religious upbringing had not succeeded in making him a practising Christian, it had branded him firmly with its morality and its masculine notions of social gentility. 'At fourteen, my world was an all male one,' he said.[2] Hence the absence of a girlfriend for Tintin (and the presence of rather too many 'Tintin and Haddock are gay' parodies in alternative comics since). Castafiore is in a different category, because she imposes her will on others. She had more in common with Adolf Hitler, say, as someone to be lampooned, than with the rest of her sex.

Hergé's views on Hitler himself are illuminating too. Like the majority of his countrymen he saw Nazism as insidious and dangerous, something to be feared. Like his countrymen, he had no real knowledge of its true nature. While *King Ottokar's Sceptre* satirised its expansion in the cleverest of ways, Tintin's junior companion strip 'Quick and Flupke' treated its readers to a direct red-nosed assault on the German leader; he was the funny chap with a little moustache, a pathetic figure of fun. After the war, however, and the discovery of the concentration camps, Hergé removed all mention of Hitler from the reprints of Quick and Flupke. Adolf was no longer funny, just disgusting. Comedy had its bounds.

In 1951, *King Ottokar's Sceptre* became the first Tintin strip to be seen by British readers, when it was serialised in *The Eagle*. Tintin retained his Belgian identity and Snowy retained his Belgian name, 'Milou'; only Dupond and Dupont had their names translated, appearing for the first time as Thompson and Thomson. The detectives' names were inherited by Michael Turner and Leslie Lonsdale-Cooper when they came to translate the stories for Methuen, starting with *King Ottokar* in 1958. A year later they also translated Hergé's 1956 semi-animated cartoon version of the story, which was broadcast on BBC Children's Television in eight episodes, beginning on 10 April 1959. Gerald Campion, the *Billy Bunter* star, provided the voice of Tintin, while Derek Guyler filled in all the other characters.

Despite its excitement value as a children's story, though, and the wit of its caricatures, *King Ottokar*'s underlying message to Hergé's countrymen was a serious one. He had enough courage to continue broadcasting his anti-Nazi convictions not only right to the end of the story, when it would have been easy to stop, but beyond that. His next story attacked the Germans directly, even though war with Germany was clearly only weeks away. That is important to remember in any final assessment of Tintin's influence on the twentieth century. The young reporter's creator may have preferred keeping his mouth shut to martyrdom during wartime; but particularly in view of his pre-war record, who can begrudge him that?

12

Land Of Black Gold

Tintin Au Pays De L'Or Noir

Before he could even begin work on *Land Of Black Gold*, the war began and Hergé was called up. He was, after all, a reservist with a French-speaking artillery company, so not unnaturally he was posted to a Flemish-speaking infantry company, in Turnhout, to the north of Belgium. There he was given what he called 'the extremely important mission' of requisitioning bicycles from farms, presumably in case they might be useful when the German panzers steamed in. Although depressed by the miseries of army life, he still managed to draw two painstaking black-and-white pages of Tintin's new adventure each week, which he posted back to the *Petit Vingtième*. Coupled with the effort involved in plotting ahead, this was no mean feat.

The story was based upon an abortive idea Hergé had dreamed up a couple of years previously, in which terrorists systematically blow up all the great buildings of Europe, starting with the Parthenon. Instead of the tourist attractions, Hergé postulated industrial sabotage. With the Allies on the eve of war, what more crippling blow than a combustible chemical inserted into petrol supplies at their Arabian source? Doctor Müller, Hergé's German villain of *The Black Island*, stage-manages the sabotage, leaving little room for doubt as to its country of origin.

Only the first twenty-seven pages of *Land Of Black Gold* now have any bearing on the story Hergé intended to write. 'I'm finishing you for good,' says Müller to the unconscious Tintin at the end of the third line on page 27.[1] In the modern version, the Thompsons arrive in the nick of time. In the *Petit Vingtième* episode of 8 May 1940, Müller ties Tintin up and leaves him in the sand to die. Slowly, the sand level rises, until only his head is visible. It was at this point that the Germans invaded Brussels, the *Petit Vingtième* closed for ever, and writing stories about international oil supplies being spiked by German villains abruptly ceased to be a safe occupation. *Land Of Black Gold*'s current incarnation is a patchwork effort, made up of various post-war adaptations and rewrites, and owing little to the story's original satirical thrust.

Between his posting in September 1939, and the German invasion eight months later, Hergé's will to carry on had been tested severely, both mentally and physically. While he and his comrades manned their requisitioned bicycles, their less-than-confident countrymen fled in droves at their backs. It must have taken a lot of guts for a Belgian soldier to stay at his post in those difficult months. Hergé, for his part, came down with a plague of boils in the new year, and was given three months' sick leave. It would be unfair at this distance to pass judgement on the medical causes of this sudden eruption; but it is difficult to forget Hergé's later capacity for bringing on psychosomatic illnesses at times of stress or unease. Whatever the reason, the boils were there sure enough. Hergé wasn't though. He'd made off to France at the first opportunity.

This was at the recommendation of Père Lou, the Chinese priest who had experienced at first hand the need for swift departures from home. He advised Hergé and his wife to make for Paris. Unfortunately, the rest of Belgium seems to have had the same idea. Paris was crammed. The unofficial confederacy of comic artists came to Hergé's aid, and an illustrator friend named Marijac lent him his farmhouse in the Auvergne. The contrast between Tintin's fearless escapades in the defence of his country and Hergé's bolt-hole in the comparative safety of the French country-side could not have been more marked. Hergé could never have been further from the protégé he had once wished to emulate, back in the days of *The Land Of The Soviets*.

Hergé did not stay in exile, though. He felt a tremendous loyalty to his country, tugging against his equally tremendous loyalty to Tintin. Above all other considerations, these two were the symbols closest to his heart. Although he had campaigned for years against the incursions of the far right, he began subscribing to the bitter belief that Belgium was being sucked against its will into a superpower conflict, between the slightly distasteful British government and the extremely distasteful German regime. All his distrust of officialdom came to the fore. So what to do next? Stay with his country, and risk the probable curtailment of Tintin's career, not to mention his own? Or abandon his homeland, taking Tintin with him to safety?

Sharing a similar emotional turmoil was the Belgian King, Léopold III, who in later years was to become a great friend of Hergé's. He had already seen Queen Wilhelmina of the Netherlands leave for London, but could not bring himself to follow suit. He was to stay with his countrymen even when the Germans came, to the anger of the French, who stripped him of his Légion d'Honneur. Eventually it was to cost him his throne. Now he made a radio appeal to all Belgians, to stay with their country through thick and thin. This included all the refugees streaming through France. At the end of June, Hergé heeded the call and went back. It must have taken more courage to return, against the tide, than to leave in the first place.

There were other artists who stayed in Brussels. E. P. Jacobs, and Jacques Van Melkebeke, both of whom worked with Hergé during the war. 'Jam' was still there too. There were scores of other trades that stayed as well, postmen, greengrocers, ironmongers, what have you; but it was the artists, along with the journalists, who were to suffer the consequences in 1944. Especially anyone connected with the *Vingtième*, even though the Germans briskly finished it off when they arrived in 1940. The Abbé Wallez retired to a monastery, which did him no good at all at the liberation. Punishing him four years later was a pointless sort of retribution; the Abbé was already a sad and disillusioned man by 1940.

Hergé found illustration work on a different newspaper, *Le Soir*, which of course was under German management now. A *Le Soir* executive, Raymond de Becker – who had commissioned Hergé to do some freelance drawings for his journal *Catholic Action* in the early 1930s – got him the job, and he settled down there. In due course, as Belgium adjusted to occupied life and all its privations, one of the things its hard-pressed citizens began to miss was Tintin. Yet was not the author of Tintin right here, still working on a Brussels newspaper? So began the next phase of Hergé's career, drawing Tintin for *Le Soir* newspaper. A special youth supplement was even created to accommodate Tintin, entitled *Le Soir Jeunesse* in memory of *Le Petit Vingtième*. Life began to take on a familiar ring.

Except, of course, Hergé had to begin work on a new story. A new type of story, come to that. By some miracle the German authorities had been too stupid to see themselves in *King Ottokar's Sceptre* or *Land Of Black Gold*, but it was not worth tempting fate any further. Hergé had done his bit to help save the world. In the words of the Taoist aphorism he found especially appropriate, 'don't look any longer for truth, just stop cherishing your opinions'. *Land Of Black Gold* was scrapped, and Hergé went back to the beginning.

So, where does the modern *Black Gold* story come from? Only pages 1 to 6 and 19 to 27 remain from the original. We must jump forward eight years, to 6 September 1948, a time when the dust of post-war recriminations has settled. Ever a meticulous man, Hergé insists that he must conclude his unfinished wartime stories before setting out on a new Tintin adventure. *Land Of Black Gold* must find a new conflict to play against. In 1948, an obvious conflict presented itself: the Jewish–Palestinian struggle in the fledgling state of Israel, and in particular the attacks on the British colonial authorities by the terrorist groups 'Irgun' and 'Stern', who opposed British attempts to appease Arab opinion by restricting Jewish immigration. This conflict would give Hergé the opportunity to extend his vague pre-war moral disapproval of colonialism, and allow for a spot of mistaken identity between Tintin and the Jewish terrorists.

So, the second version of *Land Of Black Gold* came into being. Helpfully, Tintin was already in the Middle East at the point where the first version was abandoned. True, he was tied up in a sandstorm, but that was easily solved by picking up a page earlier and saving the sandstorm scene for another five pages. The second 'Palestinian' version gave Hergé far more scope to be witty at the expense of politics, too. On the Arab side, three glorious warring factions were introduced: Sheikh Bab El Ehr (a bit player in the first version), Sheikh Ben Kalish Ezab, and the latter's dreadful little son Abdullah.

The unimaginably horrible Abdullah was the idea of Hergé's friend Jacques Van Melkebeke, modelled on the real-life Feisal II, son of King Feisal of Saudi Arabia. The gory details, though, came from a favourite pre-war character of Hergé, the tantrum-throwing Maharajah of Gopal in the Jo, Zette and Jocko adventure *Valley Of The Cobras*. Turning the Maharajah into a child, and adding a doting father, was a masterstroke. Especially memorable is the climactic scene in the underground railway tunnels of Müller's hideout, where

Tintin's mission to rescue Abdullah and return him to his father is hampered by the Prince's insistence on playing trains. To reinforce his wishes, Abdullah sinks his teeth into Tintin's hand and squirts him with soda water, at various critical life-endangering points.

Khemed, oil-rich home of this diminutive monster, is no less inventive a creation. It is Hergé's most successful imaginary country, thanks in part to its geographic accuracy, and to Hergé's remarkably realistic parody of Arab names. This pseudo-Arabic he took from Marollien, the local Brussels slang. By some curious linguistic twist, Marollien is obviously a corrupted form of English. For instance 'Bab El Ehr' is actually Marollien for 'Chatterbox', from the English 'Babbler'. 'Wadesdah', the capital of Khemed, literally means 'What is that?' Rather more obscurely, 'Kalish Ezab' derives from the Marollien words for 'Liquorice Water'.

If the transition to the new setting was handled smoothly, Hergé encountered far more problems trying to slot in his new wartime characters, Captain Haddock and Professor Calculus. The war years had changed Tintin's station in life completely. Pre-1939 he had been a solo campaigning reporter, living at No. 26 Labrador Road. In 1948 he was an adventurer-at-leisure, en-sconced as a permanent house guest in a stately home with a retired mariner and a batty professor. If he was to use the first half of the original story, Hergé could hardly explain away the absence of the Professor and the Captain without difficulty.

This is not a problem Hergé really manages to resolve. Haddock telephones on page 3 to announce he's been called up, then turns up conveniently and without explanation on page 54, to get Tintin out of a tight corner. To the end of the story, he steadfastly refuses to recount what has happened in the interim. As for the Professor, he confines himself to dropping Tintin a line on page 61, oddly enough on bright green paper. This cursory integration of the new characters is the least satisfying aspect of *Land Of Black Gold*.

Matters were to be confused still further in the late 1960s, when Methuen decided to embark on an English translation. As with *The Black Island*, the strong artistic and commercial influence of Michael Turner persuaded Hergé to redraw the book. Not, says Turner, because of the slightly unfortunate portrayal of the British, but because at that time, he and Leslie Lonsdale-Cooper feared that twenty-year-old details of the Palestinian conflict would be meaningless to a modern audience. Hergé complied, and between 1969 and 1971 a third version appeared, the version which is now available. The story was completely redrawn from the fourth line of page 6, through to page 18. Out went the Jewish terrorists, the Royal Air Force, the British mandate and all things Palestinian. In came rather more of Khemed, and with it a much improved narrative flow. Accuracy was improved too. Hergé's then assistant Bob de Moor was despatched to the Port of Antwerp to draw wartime oil tankers, something Hergé had been unable to do in 1939.

Despite these gallant efforts, *Land Of Black Gold* retains a somewhat fragmentary air. Although now officially placed fifteenth in the Tintin chronology, the story's essential characteristics are pre-war, as regards both the real and the fictional worlds it passes through. The book marks Tintin's visible retirement as a campaigning 1930s reporter. Its main protagonists – Tintin, Snowy, Müller, Oliveira da Figueira, the Thompsons – are all by nature pre-war characters, even in those sections drawn many years later.

Where it triumphs is in its comic set pieces. The Thompson twins steal the honours from under Tintin's nose, with a virtuoso performance that almost tops their *Black Island* aerobatics. After dispatching several breakdown vehicles and attempting to pass themselves off as crewmen on an oil freighter by carrying shrimp nets, they bring about a marvellous finale to their careers as chief comic diversions. Driving about in massive circles through the desert, bamboozled by mirages into colliding with the only palm tree for miles around, and donning risible red-and-white striped Victorian bathing costumes, they cap it all by swallowing Müller's petrol additive tablets and sprouting huge tufts of multi-coloured hair. Following this bizarre and spectacular episode, the two detectives tend to drift slightly into the background in later books, as Haddock and Calculus take over; but for the Thompsons as central characters, *Land Of Black Gold* is a fine swansong.

Ultimately, it is for these scenes, rather than as a work of political satire, that *Land Of Black Gold* will be remembered. During the war years, Hergé put his politics in abeyance, and they were never to surface in quite the same way again. To some, this represented collaboration; but the simple fact remains that while Europe dreamed of its freedom, and great political and military arguments raged back and forth, Hergé had been agonising over far more serious aspects of his abandoned project. For instance, do rats really live on oil tankers, as he had depicted on page 11, and if so – how do they get on board?[2]

13

The Crab With The Golden Claws

Le Crabe Aux Pinces D'Or

The Gestapo Officer was sympathetic. Hergé was, after all, a friend to the Germans. Did his artwork not decorate the flat of the Belgian Fascist leader Léon Degrelle? Ah yes. Degrelle had bought a few drawings when they had worked together on the *Vingtième*. Hergé wondered what was coming next. The reprinting of *Tintin In America* and *The Black Island* had already been halted because of their locations – had the Germans finally tumbled to *King Ottokar's Sceptre* or *Land Of Black Gold*? Or was it the toast to Hitler he had refused to drink in the nightclub? No, explained the officer. It was a little more delicate than that . . . how would Hergé like to smooth over his little publishing difficulties by becoming an informer for the Gestapo?

Any appreciation of Hergé and his work must take into account the allegation that Hergé was a Nazi sympathiser. To refuse to address the question, or to dismiss it as irrelevant, as modern-day apologists insist on doing, not only does Hergé's honesty over the matter a disservice, but ignores one of the major influences on Tintin's career. All the pre-war stories from *The Blue Lotus* on, which attack the far right, and all the wartime stories, which present a studied neutrality, are conditioned by the hostile presence of Nazism. The post-war stories, written for *Tintin* magazine, are conditioned by a lack of independence directly brought about by Hergé's wartime neutrality. The matter is fundamental to any informed understanding of the subject.

Hergé refused to become a Gestapo informant. He also refused to become the official illustrator of the Belgian Fascist movement. If he followed any political line at all it was that of the King, who himself essayed a strict neutrality while under house arrest in the confines of his own country. Yet Hergé survived, probably because Tintin was drawing readers to the Nazi-controlled *Le Soir*. On 17 October 1940, he was made editor of *Le Soir Jeunesse*. The benefit was mutual, for *Le Soir* had five times the circulation of *Le Vingtième Siècle*, and Tintin's popularity took another quantum leap.

The official line today is that Hergé was politically naive, and incapable of seeing the long-term consequences of his actions. This is almost certainly wrong. He was well aware that he would be condemned as opportunistic, if not on the wrong side altogether, and appears to have been unhappily resigned to it; but there seem to have been few alternatives open to him. He was simply taking the most honourable course available of those which included saving his skin. Although he preferred never to discuss the war in later life, those who knew him well, such as Michael Turner, will tell you that he was simply being expedient. Hergé was not a coward – he had, after all, obeyed the royal instruction to return to an occupied country. Neither was he cut out for assassinating SS men with cheesewires in dark alleys at 3 a.m. He was a comic artist who could do without politics (and vice versa) for a while.

Perhaps more than any other wartime Tintin story, *The Crab With The Golden Claws* drops politics like a hot brick. When the book version came out, Hergé quickly learnt one lesson about the impact of political satire on his audience – that they could do without it. The extended readership of *Le Soir* alone could not account for the soaring sales of *The Crab*. Relieved of the freedom to satirise political types, Hergé was now concentrating more on plot, and on developing a new style of character comedy. The public reacted positively.

The Crab With The Golden Claws is a drug mystery set in the safely neutral territory of French Morocco, a location inspired by *The White Squadron*, a novel Hergé had read in 1936. The story begins innocuously, as had been the fashion since *The Broken Ear*, when Snowy gets his nose stuck in an empty crab tin on a Brussels street. A fragment of the same tin's label turns up in the belongings of a drowned sailor, Herbert Dawes, and a mysterious Japanese policeman starts asking questions. Pretty soon Tintin is a prisoner in the hold of the *Karaboudjan*, a freighter smuggling opium, *Cigars Of The Pharaoh*-style, inside empty tins of crab. The Thompsons blunder through the story as well, on the trail of some coin counterfeiters; but pretty soon their subplot is abandoned with the introduction of a colourful new character – the drunken skipper of the *Karaboudjan*, an English sailor called Haddock.

Hergé was carefully playing with his nationalities here. Kuraki, the Japanese policeman, cautiously counterbalanced the content of *The Blue Lotus*. His two English mariners were judiciously divided, one nice, one nasty. The not so nice one was the mate, Allan, he of the 'peaked cap and Pepsodent smile' as Hergé put it, later to become Rastapopoulos' chief assistant. Allan's name in the original French was actually 'Allan Thompson', but the names Thompson and Thomson were such an inspired translation of the two detectives Dupond and Dupont, that the surname was dropped.

The nice one, Allan's skipper Haddock, was the truly inspired invention. Although Hergé was in need of characters to populate his new apolitical world, he had no idea when he devised Haddock quite how enduring the old seadog would turn out. At this stage the Captain was a long way from the stout-hearted, accident-prone companion of later adventures. He was a rather pitiful character, a manipulated, defeated old soak who drew any courage he might have from the bottle. Hergé's wife Germaine helped dream up the name over a fish dinner, when she remarked that a haddock was a 'sad English fish'. Hergé applied the name to his new character, and that is how the Captain is known the world over, except in South Africa, where the Afrikaners mysteriously refer to him as 'Captain Sardine'. Over the years the putative guest star metamorphosed into Tintin's best friend and most trustworthy companion, supplanting Snowy at his side and at the nearest whisky supply. Hergé found him more interesting to draw than a terrier. Unlike Tintin, his face was 'extremely mobile and expressive'.

Solid and bearded, Haddock's reliability grew as his temper shortened. From the first, this temper was illustrated with a devastating repertoire of insults. The idea for this went back to 1933 and the weeks following the completion of the now entirely forgotten 'Four Powers Act'. Hergé was attempting to resolve an argument between a Brussels shopkeeper and his customer, when the outraged merchant settled the matter by accusing the other of being 'a peace treaty'. The sheer irrelevance of the insult stunned his victim into defeat, and made a lasting impression on Hergé.

Haddock has two basic expletives, 'Billions of blue blistering barnacles', and 'Thundering typhoons'. The latter is a rough translation of the equally nautical-sounding 'Tonnerre de Brest', used by Haddock in the original French, and borrowed by Hergé from the uncle of his friend Marcel Stal. The litany of abuse with which Haddock greets representatives of international villain-hood, or monkeys who drop coconuts on his head, is much wider. For the most part it consists of variations on the themes of piracy, dark age barbarianism, and the early stages of man's development; but Tintinophiles may be interested in the meaning of some of Haddock's other, more obscure offerings.[1]

A Bashi-bazouk is a Turkish irregular mercenary. A Moujik is a Russian peasant. Abecedarian means 'pertaining to the alphabet', an anacoluthon is an ungrammatical sentence and a polygraph is a machine for reproducing two identical drawings at once. A

slubberdegullion is a dirty, worthless fellow, a jobber-
nowl is an idiot, a poltroon is a coward, a picaroon is a
rogue, a troglodyte lives in a cave, an anthropophagus
eats people and a pyrographer practises poker-work.
Colocynth is bitter-apple, phylloxera is a plant-louse
injurious to vines, and a pachyrhizus is a plant with thick
roots. An ophicleide is a musical instrument. A macro-
cephalic baboon has a long head. A cyclotron is an
apparatus for the electromagnetic acceleration of atomic
nuclei, while a cercopithecus is, naturally enough, a
genus of long-tailed African monkey with calluses on its
buttocks.

Hergé combed dictionaries and reference works for
suitable words, which had to be threatening-sounding
but innocuous. Only once did he make a mistake, when
he used the word 'clysopump', a rather graphic medical
term to do with the bowel. His one-time friend and
collaborator Jacques Van Melkebeke was quick to
follow this up, forging a letter from an irate father,
which complained that his small son had been permanently corrupted. Hergé was taken in completely, as he
always was by practical jokes, and was not let in on
the secret until he had composed a suitably abject reply.

As the years went by, Hergé fed the characters of
others into the Captain. Soon, Haddock was clearly
exhibiting the characteristics of Hergé's colourist E. P.
Jacobs, described by Hergé as 'full of movement, hearty,
then bursting into invective'.[2] Some of his bluffness
came from Bob de Moor. The most important ingredient of all, though, was Hergé himself. There is no
doubt that Hergé began increasingly to articulate his

own desires through the Captain – which essentially amounted to a quiet life, free from parrots and fat opera singers. Many of the incidents which befell Haddock at Marlinspike were drawn from Hergé's own life.

If the cast list of *The Crab With The Golden Claws* was growing, the space in which the characters operated was shrinking dramatically. *Le Soir Jeunesse* was a large piece of paper folded in quarters to make eight pages, of which Tintin occupied two as before. In May 1941, this shrunk to one page, as the war on the Russian front bit into the economy, and thus into paper supplies. On 23 September *Le Soir Jeunesse* was scrapped altogether, and Tintin moved to a daily four-frame strip in the main paper. The cramped conditions in which Tintin had to work can still be seen in some of the frames. On page 15 of the book, for instance, when Tintin is trying to escape from the *Karaboudjan*, a thin strip has obviously been added to the top of each frame: the ship's rivets give out a few millimetres short.

This change in working methods forced Hergé to redesign the story's latter stages in a more staccato style. As a result of all this chopping and changing, *The Crab With The Golden Claws* became the only Tintin adventure too short for the current 62-page format. Fortunately, four painted colour plates had been added to each of the black-and-white Tintin books except *Soviets*, from 1936 onwards. As *The Crab* was fifty-eight pages in length, four pages short, when the time came to colour it, all Hergé had to do was redraw the four plates as full-page frames. That these larger drawings were added later can be seen by their thicker line and richer colours.

The book underwent further slight revision after the war at the demand of its American editors, who ironically displayed more intolerance than the Nazis had ever done. Hergé was forced to cut out illustrations of Haddock drinking on page 19, and to change two members of Allan's multiracial gang into white men: Jumbo, the crewman first seen on page 14, and the man seen beating Captain Haddock on page 53. Unfortunately – or perhaps mischievously – Hergé forgot to alter the text as well. At the top of page 58, Haddock can clearly be seen urging the police to 'Arrest that negro!' as a white man flies past.

It was while working on *The Crab With The Golden Claws* that Hergé first met Edgar P. Jacobs, the colourist who was to breathe life into all the early adventures a few years later. Hergé seems to have made few really deep friendships; despite his remarkable social ease he was a reserved man, and the reminiscences of those who knew him are the reminiscences of close colleagues rather than close friends. At the same time, he disliked loneliness, and the company of his wife – who at times seems to have been more like the chief of his supporters' club – was not enough to dispel the isolation he had been feeling since he started his freelance career.

So it was that as 1940 turned into 1941, he took another collaborator, the humorist Jacques Van Melkebeke, to work not so much on the Tintin stories as on other projects. Together they wrote a play, *Tintin In The Indies* or *The Mystery Of The Blue Diamond*. Obviously, Hergé was still unable to decide between enigmatic titles and the 'Tintin and . . .'

variety! Covering much the same ground as the second half of *Cigars Of The Pharaoh*, it concerned Tintin's hunt for, and discovery of, the stolen blue diamond of the Maharajah of Padakhore.

The piece premiered at the Théâtre Royal des Galeries St Hubert in Brussels on 15 April 1941, where it ran for three days, and then for a further week from 1 May. Surprisingly it was a musical, and Tintin – androgynously – was played by a girl, Jeanne Rubens, in true panto tradition (the supply of young men being less than plentiful during wartime). Sadly, no trace of the play now remains – or indeed of the short animated film version of *The Crab* that Hergé made after the war – save for a few decent reviews. The director, Paul Riga, and the composer, Henri Colas, do not seem to have stamped their names on theatrical history either, which may have something to do with it. At any rate, the play was good enough to beget a successor.

Curiously, Hergé and Melkebeke chose to change the stage names of the two detectives, from Dupond and Dupont to Durand and Durant. This caused a great deal of confusion at *Le Soir*, where a sub who had presumably seen a review of the play started billing them as Durand and Durant in the newspaper strip proper soon afterwards. The mix-up does not seem to have bothered Melkebeke's childhood friend Jacobs, who watched the first night and enjoyed it immensely. He was introduced to Hergé afterwards as an opera singer with a taste for illustration and colouring on the side, and the two got on famously. It was not long before their talents were harnessed.

For the moment, however, Hergé had to write and draw the next Tintin strip alone. It would be a maritime adventure, he was sure of that, so that Haddock's services could be retained. Like *The Crab*, it had to be studiously neutral. To some extent though, Tintin's adventures in North Africa had proved themselves innocent under scrutiny; now Hergé could afford to experiment a little. His next story would cautiously advance a few political theories, which, if well disguised, might pass unnoticed by the wrong sort of people . . .

14

The Shooting Star

L'Etoile Mystérieuse

The Mysterious Star, as it is known in the original French, is the most important of all Hergé's wartime stories. It expounds his own unusual political philosophies, and moreover it was the main document by which he was adversely judged after the war. Ostensibly, it follows the escapist pattern of *The Crab With The Golden Claws*; an international plot, good guys v. bad guys, and no politics in sight. Yet there is an air of bizarre fantasy about the story which does not tally with anything that Hergé had produced before.

The early settings are grey, the style downbeat, elements familiar to anyone living in occupied Brussels. This bleak background is the scene of a near-apocalyptic event: a giant meteor is heading straight for the earth, about to bring an end to civilisation. Instead, the meteor veers away harmlessly, leaving behind it an illusory earth tremor and a slab of meteorite in the Arctic Ocean. Immediately, Tintin and Haddock sign up for the European scientific expedition to find the meteorite; but there is American opposition. Even before Tintin's ship the SS *Aurora* sets sail for the frozen north, someone from the rival expedition attempts to dynamite her. Fortunately Snowy defuses the situation, in a repeat of his leg-cocking exploit later deleted from *Cigars Of The Pharaoh*.

Add to this a fearsome giant spider that turns out to be a tiny one walking across an observatory telescope lens, and a prophet of doom who turns out to be barking mad, and the atmosphere becomes quite eerie. Hergé did not normally go in for hidden meanings, preferring to score points with humour, and he disliked critical analysis that pointed to such meanings where they did not exist. Wartime, however, was a special case, and for once he allowed himself an illicit dose of symbolism. The giant meteor represented the war itself, a terrible apparition capable of destroying life, limb and property, but ultimately something that would pass by without lasting damage. After the war, Hergé believed, there would grow up in due course a new rivalry, between America and a United Europe. This was the Abbé Wallez's old philosophy coming through again. The rivalry was represented by the two expeditions' naval race to the Arctic.

The way things are going in Europe, Hergé may yet be proved right. Although it is a touch fanciful to suggest, as some have done, that he also predicted the discovery of atomic weapons. True, the meteorite was comprised of strange metals, capable of mutating life, and highly explosive in a mushroom-shaped way; but when he drew the story no one had yet exploded an atomic bomb and discovered its effects. Hergé was an intelligent man, but not prescient. His mushrooms did, after all, have large pretty red spots.

Trouble arose, indirectly, through Hergé's decision to make the bad guys American. He did not dislike Americans per se; his views were not that generalised. 'I saw no signs of anti-Americanism,' says Michael Turner of his 25-year relationship with Hergé. Yet Hergé's distaste for American big business was indisputable. Writing in a city crawling with German soldiers, US commercial interests must have seemed a safe bet to cast in the role of unscrupulous opposition. With hindsight though, it was a tactless decision.

Critics point to the nationalities of the scientists in the pan-European party, all from neutral or axis countries: a Belgian, a Frenchman, a German, a Spaniard, a Swede and a Portuguese. Was this not tantamount to Nazi propaganda? Actually, this is unjustified criticism. There were only two countries left in Europe by 1941 that were not either neutral or occupied. One was Russia, as Asian as it was European, and anathema to all Belgians; the other was Britain, and there was already a Briton with the party in the shape of Haddock. Furthermore another Briton, the splendid Captain Chester, does the party a good turn on the dockside at Reykjavik, when the Americans attempt to put a block on the *Aurora*'s petrol supply.

For their part, the Americans were less than overjoyed at being cast in the black hats, and in 1954 Hergé had to change the nationality of his evil money men. He shifted their base a continent southwards, to the fictitious republic and undoubtedly comfortable tax haven of São Rico. Today both the 'European Foundation For Scientific Research' vessel and its São Rico counterpart can be seen flying rather similar red and black flags. To give the game away, though, the opposition boat is still named after the American polar explorer Robert Peary.

Far worse resulted, however, from the name Hergé gave to his chief cigar-puffing American financier. Knowing little about the USA, he borrowed a typical American tycoon's name, 'Blumenstein'. In the nick of time, someone more knowledgeable than he pointed out the Jewish connotations of this name. Relieved, Hergé had time to change it before the story went to press. He reverted instead to the Brussels slang which always stood him in such good stead. A bollewinkel, a Brussels sweet-pastry shop, sounded about right, especially when it was Americanised to Bohlwinkel. The story went into *Le Soir* that week featuring a fat cigar-puffing financier called Bohlwinkel, which – as someone even more knowledgeable pointed out, too late – was actually a common Jewish name as well. By a disastrous accident, Tintin was escorting a German professor and his colleagues to the Arctic, to defeat the forces of the international Jewish financial conspiracy.

It was the sort of terminal blunder that tended to obscure all high-minded notions of united European scientific research in a free post-war world. Hergé never quite lived it down, although as a genuinely innocent mistake he stoutly refused to alter it. Not that matters came to a head until the liberation, though. For the time being, retribution was some way off. He had got his frozen north adventure out of the way, and his valuable meteorite idea, as well as banging the drum for a few of the Abbé's old theories that he happened to agree with.

In the short term, there were other advantages to *The Shooting Star*. If paper was in short supply in wartime Brussels, ink was not. It was time for Tintin to move into colour at last. *The Shooting Star* is the first Tintin story conceived entirely from the start as a 62-page, four lines per page colour adventure – the old, rambling, 180-page, three lines per page black-and-white stories were finished for ever. The new limitations seemed to improve the stories – a stimulant, rather than a restriction. 'I am more at my ease in a precise format,' confessed Hergé later, looking back and comparing his work before and after *The Shooting Star*.

Hergé's publisher Louis Casterman was delighted with the opportunity to move into colour, and decided that all the old books should immediately be redrawn, rewritten and relettered as well. Hergé set about the task with gusto, if not with enough skill for his own liking, and coloured *The Crab With The Golden Claws*, *The Broken Ear* and *The Black Island* first. Of these, his tentatively pale colours suited the Saharan sands of *The Crab*, if not the lush jungles of *The Broken Ear*. The wartime version of *The Black Island* did not last, while Hergé was sufficiently dissatisfied with *The Shooting Star* to recolour it completely a few years later.

The story of *The Shooting Star* does not throw up any lasting characters, although Captain Chester of the *Sirius*[1] and Professor Cantonneau are referred to briefly in later books. Hergé is too busy establishing Haddock as Tintin's right-hand man, in a number of excellent sequences. Best of all is the scene where he greets Chester on the Icelandic quayside with an aggressive-looking naval ritual: 'Fidgy! Fidgy! Fidgy! Boodle, boodle, boodle! Aye, aye, ayeyeeé! Dear old Chester! Just the same as ever!' Then there is his attempt to drink a tonic water a few pages later, containing the biggest 'thimbleful' of whisky the world has ever seen. Hergé's own favourite scene was the stormy dinner on the *Aurora*, where the multitude of professors turn progressively greener and troop out in a line to moan in their bunks.

Professor Decimus Phostle is the Calculus-prototype loopy professor on offer this time around, but there was one more model constructed before the advent of the real thing. On 26 December 1941 Hergé and Melkebeke's second Tintin play, the script of which is – like its predecessor – now missing, opened at the Théâtre des Galeries. It was called *The Disappearance Of Mr Bullock*, and featured the same production crew as before, although this time there was a male Tintin – Roland Navez – and the Dupond/ts got their names back. The story took Tintin to China, Tibet, Morocco, Brazil and Argentina, but the chief attraction appears to have been a batty professor named Dory-Ford. A doryphore, incidentally, was one of Haddock's range of insults.[2]

Hergé took a short break before embarking upon his next story. It was to be a double-length extravaganza, with the mad professor to end all mad professors. It was also going to steer clear of politics and symbolism. It was going to be yet another maritime adventure, because the Captain was too good a character to leave out, and it was going to differ from *The Shooting Star* in one other important respect. The *Aurora* had been drawn from Hergé's imagination, as a visit to the docks for 'research purposes' would probably have ended in front of the firing squad. As the Arctic voyage had unfolded, experienced mariners quickly pointed out that the vessel would have been hard pressed to stay afloat for more than ten minutes. So, the boat at the centre of his next book would be perfect in every detail. It would be seaworthy, robust and fine-looking. It would also be three hundred years old and eighteen inches high.

15

The Secret Of The Unicorn

Le Secret De La Licorne

The war, it might be said, marks the third, or central stage of Tintin's career. The wartime Tintin stories carry a completely different emphasis, through harsh necessity, from their predecessors. Yet in 1942, the lessons of *The Shooting Star*, and the need to avoid offending the various people who were queuing up to be offended, led Hergé to institute a sea-change in Tintin's life so dramatic as to transcend all such distinctions. Hergé had embarrassed himself on *The Shooting Star*, and change had to be implemented quickly.

The Secret Of The Unicorn – Red Rackham's Treasure duology was Hergé's first double-length story since *Cigars Of The Pharaoh* and *The Blue Lotus* ten years before, and the transformation it brought about in Tintin's life was equally radical. It was here that Tintin's days as a boy reporter drifted to an end.[1] Reporters are not popular during wartime, especially those with a long history of intrepid political reportage for the other side. Tintin's journalist-as-newsmaker reporting belonged firmly to the pre-war tradition anyway. For the time being at least, Tintin would become an explorer instead.

Exploring was a profession that combined the traditional Tintin virtues of bravery and derring-do with
locations that would not raise any eyebrows at Gestapo
headquarters, and characters that would not tread on
anybody's toes, even accidentally. Expeditions could be
mounted to hunt for treasure, to rescue friends, or just
to discover the odd new planet or two. For appearances'
sake, Tintin would continue to be called a reporter, but
in practice his notebook and pencil were set aside for
good in 1942. Perhaps for sentiment's sake, he was
allowed one last phonecall to his editor, in a sequence
that never appeared in the book version, to brief him on
the developing *Secret Of The Unicorn*.

There was no tearstained parting with his landlady,
Mrs Finch. No doubt she was getting a little fed up with
seeing foreigners kidnapped or shot on her doorstep, or
her rooms being blown up by bowler-hatted detectives.
Tintin's lifestyle had to change, though, and No. 26
Labrador Road became a part of his past. In its place
came a stately home, a butler, and an inexhaustible
supply of money. Haddock had to come along too, of
course. Hergé couldn't go on inventing stories about
ships for ever, just to include him.

All in all it was a complicated state of affairs to bring
about; but even if the transition did take two books to
complete, it was achieved with apparent effortlessness.
To date, the two-part treasure hunt is the most successful of all the Tintin adventures. More people have read
Red Rackham's Treasure than any other Tintin story,
often without realising that *The Secret Of The Unicorn* is
an equally good, if not better book. Until the intensely

personal *Tintin In Tibet* was published in 1960, Hergé himself rated the *Unicorn* as his best work.

Although the two books form one adventure, they could not be more different. *Red Rackham's Treasure* is a lush travelogue, the first of the series of post-war fantasies we now think of as classic Tintin. *The Secret Of The Unicorn* belongs unquestionably to the 1930s, in style, colour and content. It is the last and best of Hergé's detective mysteries, taking place – for the first time – entirely in Belgium, almost as if the old Tintin were having a last look around the Brussels streets. Only the country-house games of *The Castafiore Emerald* were to keep Tintin and Haddock at home for a whole 62 pages again.

The *Unicorn* has three plot strands, which needless to say converge neatly at the end and lead into *Red Rackham's Treasure*. First, there is Tintin's hunt for three identical models of a seventeenth-century warship *The Unicorn*, each model containing part of a treasure map rolled in its mast. Secondly, the Thompson twins are following the trail of Aristides Silk, a pickpocket with a bureaucratic obsession for filing wallets that comes in useful at the finish. Finally, there is the Haddock element, a stroke of genius. The Captain appears to have gone mad, barricaded inside his flat. In fact, he is merely reliving the exploits of his ancestor Sir Francis Haddock, captain of the sunken *Unicorn*, assisted by a bottle of rum or five. In the middle of the detective story comes a full-scale late seventeenth-century naval encounter, planned and executed with remarkable historical detail.[2]

Hergé created his *Unicorn* by combining two French ships of the period, the *Brilliant* and the *Soleil Royale*, together with a later English frigate that possessed a unicorn figurehead. His pirate chief, Red Rackham, was a real person – Jean Rackham, who had seized control of his ship in 1718 from another pirate captain, Charles Vane, only to be caught and hanged two years later. While the battle rages in (almost) a serious vein, Haddock's narrative provides the comic relief. 'When Sir Francis came round he found himself securely lashed to his own mast. He suffered terribly.' Tintin: 'From that blow on the head, of course . . .' Haddock, a look of distant despair in his eyes: 'No, from thirst!' (He promptly drains another tumbler of rum at a single gulp.)

Hergé was to use this device repeatedly, where Haddock plays the fool to smooth over a lengthy explanation. In *The Red Sea Sharks*, when Tintin is explaining the plot to Oliveira da Figueira, Haddock falls asleep and sets fire to his beard with his pipe. In *Destination Moon*, when Hergé was perhaps guilty of being too proud of the thoroughness of his research, Chief Engineer Wolff is bombarding Haddock and Tintin with radioactive theory. 'When an atom of U.235 splits, it releases two or three neutrons. One or other of these will be absorbed by an atom of U.238, which will thus be transmuted into plutonium. But those other neutrons? Where will they go?' Haddock: 'Yes . . . I'm worried about them . . .' 'Restricted by the graphite that surrounds them, they continue through the pile, and end up by hitting one of the rare atoms of U.235. These

THE SECRET OF THE UNICORN

in their turn split and release two or three neutrons again . . . You see?' Haddock: 'Of course: It's child's play.'

For reasons of time, such meticulous research had usually been beyond Hergé during the 1930s, and the good intentions of *The Blue Lotus* had been dissipated somewhat; but in 1942, at the time of *Secret Of The Unicorn*, he had less work on his hands, and was able to start researching his stories with a thoroughness that became his trademark. As the years went by, he became almost obsessive in the pursuit of detail. As with *King Ottokar's Sceptre*, events tended to prove Hergé's more carefully researched stories right, and this was certainly the case with the two Rackham books.

Carlsen, the Danish publisher,[3] discovered a ship called the *Enhjørningen*, a real–life *Unicorn* built in 1605 that was very similar to Hergé's vessel. Then, astonishingly, Sir Francis Haddock turned out to have genuine counterparts as well – a whole family of them, boasting seven Captains and two Admirals among their number. The seventeenth–century Haddocks of Leigh–on–Sea seem to have shared the Captain's family traditions of bravery tempered with incompetence. Admiral Sir Richard Haddock, for instance, gallantly sent his warship *The Royal James* to the bottom at the battle of Sole Bay, while one of the many Captain Haddocks got himself court-martialled in 1674.

Haddock is the only regular character whose relatives turn up in the Tintin stories at all (if one discounts Wagg, whose family is part of his unique appeal).[4] His long and distinguished ancestry was necessary for the plot, to provide a suitable ancestral home for Tintin and himself to move into. This was Marlinspike Hall, or 'Moulinsart' in the original French, a name created by transposing the syllables of the Belgian town of Sarmoulin. In fact it was the famous château of Cheverny, shorn of its two great wings. If Tintin, Haddock and the other characters manage to be truly international, Marlinspike will never be anything but a Loire château with the ends sawn off.

Hergé had Marlinspike vacated and ready for occupation. With it came Nestor, the hexagonal-headed butler, a man possessed of admirable dexterity in packing suitcases at speed, endless reserves of patience in dealing with misdirected telephone calls for Cutts the butcher, and a large collection of starched collars. All that was needed for an idyllic lifestyle was enough money to hire Nestor and buy Marlinspike, one more character to help populate it, and a limitless supply of cash with which to live there. The great treasure hunt was underway, and Hergé made straight for the shipbuilder's yard at Ostend fishing port. He needed the complete building specifications of a typical trawler, from which to build himself a detailed scale model. Haddock and Tintin were not putting to sea in an unworkable boat this time.

16

Red Rackham's Treasure

Le Trésor De Rackham Le Rouge

Abruptly, *Red Rackham's Treasure* abandons the complex plotting of *The Secret Of The Unicorn*, in favour of an episodic style of adventure not seen since the early books; but this is not a retrograde step. For the complexity of the characters' relationships increases in inverse proportion to the plot detail, carrying the bulk of the humour with it. Furthermore the element of suspense, provided by one or two unanswered questions, holds the whole thing together. Will Tintin find the treasure? Who is the mysterious stowaway who has eaten the cook's biscuits, stolen the Thompsons' bedding, and filled Haddock's whisky crates with steel plating?

The answer to the latter is, of course, Cuthbert Calculus. Hergé had found the third and final member of the Tintin 'family'. Although he didn't know it at the time (like Haddock, Calculus was originally intended as a one-off) his eleven-year quest to find the perfect absent-minded professor was over. Constant trial and error had produced a great comic creation whose inability to hear anything said to him correctly defeated even the strongest-willed resistance. It takes a deft touch indeed to make a deaf old man funny, rather than pitiable. Calculus' secret was that Hergé never once took away his dignity.

Calculus's original French name is Tryphon Tournesol, the surname meaning (rather inappropriately) 'sunflower'. The Christian name was borrowed from an absent-minded carpenter who did a job for Hergé and forgot to present his bill. The real role model, however, was Professor Auguste Piccard, the equally dignified and eccentric inventor of the bathyscaphe – a deep-sea observation vessel not entirely unlike Calculus' submarine, albeit a little less shark-shaped. Hergé occasionally saw Piccard in the street in Brussels: 'He seemed the very incarnation of a Professor.' Piccard was, unlike Calculus, immensely tall. 'I had to scale him down, or else I'd have had to make the frames bigger.'[1]

Calculus was to mishear virtually everything said to him for the next thirty years. Only in the moon adventure, when the Syldavians temporarily fix him up with a hearing aid, is this pattern interrupted. Presumably they take it back at the end of the story, for he never wears it again. It's then that we finally discover his remarkably short temper and his pronounced aversion to the word 'goat'. For a brief period the professor becomes an important and powerful scientific figure, as first he masterminds the moon expedition and then invents the all-powerful sonic weapon in *The Calculus Affair*. After that he returns to his original role of potty inventor, developing an entirely hopeless pair of motorised rollerskates in *The Red Sea Sharks* and, in 1962, a retina-scorching version of colour television for *The Castafiore Emerald* – although his hackles still rise when anyone mentions a certain bearded brown-grey mammal.

In *Red Rackham's Treasure* Calculus' shark submarine proves entirely unhelpful, needless to say, in locating the pirate's booty. Interestingly, the useless machine was not Hergé's idea but a genuine if short-lived German wartime invention that he had spotted in a news photograph. There are other pieces of real life in there too: the *Sirius* of course (no relation to Captain Chester's boat in *The Shooting Star*) was actually a trawler called the *John*, drawn from the model built after Hergé's visit to Ostend docks. The tribal effigy of Sir Francis Haddock that Tintin finds on the island was based on a real museum piece, a Bamileke tribal fetish from Cameroon, although the African version was much smaller.

Students of Hergé's technique might be interested to know that *Red Rackham's Treasure* contains one of the two drawings that he considered to be his best ever. The other is in *The Crab With The Golden Claws*. They are unusual and revealing choices. The drawing from *Red Rackham*, the first frame on page 25, appears to be a fairly commonplace illustration showing Haddock striding up the beach, while Tintin and the Thompsons pull their skiff on to the sand. The trawler lies at anchor in the background. The drawing from *The Crab* – the second frame on page 38 – is similarly commonplace. Startled Arab raiders begin to peel away from their sand dune and flee into the distance, as a stream of enraged invective floats into the frame from the rapidly approaching Haddock.

Hergé liked them both so much because in one frame they encapsulate an entire sequence of events, advancing the plot rapidly and explicitly. Aesthetic considerations are kept to a minimum. It is not impossible that Hergé was being a trifle disingenuous when he awarded these frames such an accolade – he did have a tendency to toy with his questioners. ('How do you see yourself after all these years?' 'In a mirror.') Yet whether he genuinely meant it or not, he certainly wished to make it plain to the outside world that storytelling was his prime consideration, and that artistry would and should be subjugated to that end.

By *Red Rackham's Treasure* Hergé had none the less attained a high technical standard as an illustrator, tempered by his need to draw a strip every day and by a slight amateurishness with colour. Although this was the third book ostensibly drawn with colour in mind from the start, it still had to be drawn in black-and-white for the newspaper first. As a result the colour tends to come in slightly clumsy slabs. Many of the pages are more aesthetically pleasing in black-and-white: page 32, for instance, which has only three basic colours. The picture of Calculus surfacing in the bottom left-hand corner is a perfect example of an illustration that looks as if colour was added as an afterthought. It is a pity, because Hergé's composition is showing more signs of imagination than before. The gentle rolling of the ship on pages 16–19 is almost subliminal, but influences the whole scene.

At this stage Hergé was working almost exclusively in two sizes of shot, as it were: head to toe and head to waist. After the war, when he carved out more time for himself to compose illustrations, he experimented with more cinematic framings. He also drew every frame from different angles, often with scores of variations only millimetres apart, before choosing the composition that best suited the frame and the advancement of the story. If this was the pure distillation of function, then the results were often surprisingly beautiful.

Hergé's emphasis on propelling the story forward obviously paid off in the case of *Red Rackham's Treasure*, which attained its exalted place as Tintin's best-selling adventure almost immediately upon publication. So popular was it, that in 1952 the two Rackham stories were chosen by Casterman to become the first Tintin books to be published in England, seven years before the Leslie Lonsdale-Cooper–Michael Turner editions so well known today. Published in a different translation to the current one, under the Casterman imprint, the books sank without trace: no doubt the difficulties of mounting a campaign on foreign soil proved too much for the Belgian publishers. *The Secret Of The Unicorn* and *Red Rackham's Treasure* soon appeared in Britain again, successfully this time, as two of the earliest of the current versions; but anyone who finds a copy of either English Casterman edition on a dusty bookshelf will find themselves very rich indeed.

Certainly Tintin and Haddock found themselves very rich, after an ingenious twist in the plot finally led them to Red Rackham's hoard; although few people remember that it was actually Calculus, with the patent money on his submarine, who actually bought (and therefore became the owner of) Marlinspike. The three of them were now set up for life, in a luxurious existence probably even more enviable than Tintin's former lifestyle. Hergé himself saw it that way, through the Haddock persona. Unfortunately, barely had the idyll begun when it was threatened with extinction. The German occupiers of Belgium, whose attentions the whole exercise had been designed to avoid, found themselves losing their grip.

17

The Seven Crystal Balls

Les Sept Boules De Cristal

Hergé began the last of his wartime stories, *The Seven Crystal Balls*, on 16 December 1943. Before it finally drew to a close in March 1948, over four years later, he was to experience the greatest upheaval of his life.

The new story was another two-part apolitical fantasy, intended to reproduce the success of the *Rackham* books. Again, the first part would outline the mystery and the object of the hunt, and the second part would tell the story of the expedition. Whereas the *Rackham* books had really been two separate stories linked by a single theme, *The Seven Crystal Balls–Prisoners Of The Sun* duology became Hergé's first genuine and homogeneous long story.

The mystery was not a mystery in the *Unicorn* sense, of a plot to be unravelled, more a mystery in the Tutankhamun mould. Fear of the unknown is the over-riding theme of *The Seven Crystal Balls*. Seven explorers break open an Inca tomb in Peru; in the weeks that follow their triumphant return home, each falls into a deep coma, with just one clue to their condition – the shattered fragments of a crystal ball found beside each body. The eighth victim, Professor Calculus himself, is kidnapped at the house of his friend Professor Tarragon during an electric storm. The Thompsons, meanwhile, blunder their way through the case, failing to protect each of the scientists in turn. The humour and menace are well blended as usual, but *The Seven Crystal Balls* is undoubtedly Hergé's most frightening book.

This atmosphere of unease accumulates steadily from misleadingly comic beginnings. Tintin has not actually moved into Marlinspike yet; left to his own devices, Haddock has developed a preposterous lord of the manor act, involving jodhpurs, monocles, refined manners and recalcitrant horses that insist on coming home without him. The remaining shreds of his dignity disappear backstage at the Hippodrome Theatre, where he manages to get his own head trapped inside a giant bull's head, finishing up ingloriously in the orchestra pit via the stage. The completion of the Captain's transition from the pitiable drunk of *The Crab With The Golden Claws* to chief sidekick and comic attraction is further emphasised by the abrupt decline that Snowy has gone through. The talking wonderdog of the 1930s is now a barking, cat-chasing bundle of fur, who forces Nestor into a heroic balancing act with the drinks tray; in other words, a normal dog.

Various familiar faces turn up in *The Seven Crystal Balls*. A muted General Alcazar is appearing at the Hippodrome, nine years on from *The Broken Ear*, reduced now to a stage knife-throwing act. Bianca Castafiore also makes her second appearance in the

Tintin series, ruffling Haddock's new hairstyle and Tintin's pink tie at fifty paces with the Jewel Song from *Faust*. As with *Cigars Of The Pharaoh*, the unusual order in which the English translations were published necessitates a bit of juggling: Tintin has to refer back to *The Calculus Affair* and *The Red Sea Sharks*, adventures which have not happened yet. The other character to recur here is Professor Paul Cantonneau from *The Shooting Star*, although to be fair he is less of a character than a highly entertaining moustache.

The theatre scene is a masterpiece of detail that would not have been possible without the extra time afforded by *Le Soir's* increasingly stuttering production schedule, and the extra pair of hands provided by Hergé's new colleague. Jacobs was on board now, as of New Year's Day 1944, and although he had been taken on as a colourist he also helped to write and draw *The Seven Crystal Balls*. Since meeting him at the first night of *The Blue Diamond* in 1941, Hergé's friendship with the neat, dark little illustrator had grown, and he had come to know and admire Jacobs' meticulous work for the magazine *Bravo*. Towards the end of 1943 Hergé formally asked him to go into partnership.

The tribulations of the war combined with the loneliness of his solo career hung heavy on Hergé, who was no longer the carefree youth who had railed wittily against the world during the 1930s. He was as glad of Jacobs' companionship as of his skill with colours. Although Hergé retained his sense of humour, he had become a quiet, cautious, meticulous man, which seemed to match Jacobs' character. The artist Jacques

Martin, who worked with both men later, described how the two of them would sit together, polishing and repolishing a phrase here, taking out a word there, then maybe putting it back in again. 'When E. P. Jacobs worked with Hergé, one could say they rivalled each other in their thoroughness . . . they were supremely unhurried.'

Together they researched and drew a number of passages, including the theatre scene. The hideous mummy of Rascar Capac that attacks Tintin in his nightmare, brandishing a crystal ball, was actually a Peruvian Paracas mummy from the same collection that yielded the Haddock idol in *Red Rackham*. Professor Tarragon's house in the forest was in reality a large house on a suburban street in Boitsfort, chosen by Jacobs for its character. It later turned out to be an SS garrison building, which could have proved embarrassing had either of them been caught sketching it.

After Calculus has been kidnapped from Tarragon's house, and the comatose scientists have gone into seizure on what is now page 49, Tintin and Haddock were to have turned their attentions northward, searching the Belgian coast for traces of the Professor; but in September 1944, the war passed back the way it had come, and the Allies entered Brussels. Hergé's German employers at *Le Soir* fled, and three days later on the 6th, all employees of the newspaper were officially sacked. Two days after that, the Allied High Command extended the order. Anyone employed by the occupied press in any capacity was banned from working.

Hergé and Jacobs were arrested as traitors, and

thrown into jail. *The Shooting Star* and the *Vingtième* connection only made matters worse. It was the last anyone was to see of Tintin for two years. Hergé could have hidden, or fled, but there was no point. This moment was inevitable. He had been anticipating it for some time.

Disgraced and unemployable, Hergé passed in and out of police hands four times. He was arrested by three resistance groups, a different group picking him up each time another one let him go. He was hardly alone in this. Gangs roamed the streets, attacking the houses of anyone who could be accused of collaboration. Jamin and his family were arrested, as was Melkebeke. The Abbé Wallez was picked up at his monastery. Of course, things were much worse for him – his trials continued well into the 1950s. In the hysterical atmosphere, wild and stupid charges were brought against the Abbé. He was accused of hiding a German radio transmitter in his high altar, of taking his hunting rifle along to support his local German ack-ack battery, and of sheltering no less a person than Mussolini in his room (difficult, as only Mussolini's photograph had actually left Italy). The small patch of rapeseed in his garden was held up as evidence that he had supplied fuel to the Luftwaffe.

The ferocity of this reaction to the pre-war Catholic right did not spare even the King. Although he had spent the war as a prisoner of the Germans, Léopold was now forced into exile in Switzerland. It was not until 1950 that a referendum was held, asking the Belgians if they wanted their monarch back. The country's huge Catholic majority voted a resounding yes, but the opposition was so vociferous in defeat that Léopold chose to avoid the rancour altogether. He handed the throne on to his son, Baudouin.

For their part, Hergé and Jacobs had to work anonymously to live, disguising their drawing style heavily under the name 'Olav'. All their spare time was spent colouring and redesigning the Tintin stories for a brighter day to come.[1] Hergé did not complain, but remained bitter at the treatment meted out to those who – as he saw it – had stuck with Belgium in her hour of need. In fact, it was the very neutrality he mutely believed to be a virtue of his wartime work that was being held against him.

A parody cartoon strip entitled *The Adventures Of Tintin And Snowy In The Land Of The Nazis* started up in the newspaper *La Patrie*. So what if Hergé had attacked Nazis before the war? Did not Germans and Englishmen stand side by side for the good of mankind in the Tintin books? A scientist from Munich had helped to find *The Shooting Star*, and in the Belgian version of *The Seven Crystal Balls* the Sanders-Hardiman party was known as the Sanders-Hardmuth expedition. This even-handedness was widely – perhaps deliberately – misinterpreted as a positive enthusiasm for things German; something of a career-limiting move in 1944.

The little pointers to his true feelings that Hergé had included in the stories escaped the liberators' notice, just as the Germans had never noticed points scored at their expense either. For instance, nobody in a *Le Soir* Tintin adventure ever read *Le Soir*. They all read *La Depêche* instead, immortalised for British readers as *The Daily*

Reporter. It didn't matter. Tintin was finished, unless Hergé could get a 'certificate of good citizenship', without which he was barred from working. The chances of that happening were minimal. There seemed no one who could help. Until suddenly, at the end of 1945, after a year of ostracism and loneliness, help arrived out of the blue.

18

Prisoners Of The Sun

Le Temple Du Soleil

Two years after *The Seven Crystal Balls* has been interrupted on page 49, Tintin walks up the steps of Marlinspike on page 50. 'Good afternoon, Nestor. How is the Captain?' 'Oh sir, he's aged ten years since this trouble began. And you, sir? Have you any news?' 'None, Nestor.' Upstairs, slumped in an armchair in his dressing gown, scowling depressively at the world, is Haddock. Suddenly the telephone rings. Haddock answers. 'Hello . . . yes it's me . . . Who's that? . . . Oh? . . . Well, what news? . . . What?!' In a trice he is out of the chair and striding towards the door. 'Blistering barnacles, let's go!' he exclaims. Tintin rushes after him, hurrying to keep up.

In real life, of course, the man in the armchair was Hergé, and the telephone call, which came towards the end of 1945, was from the publisher Raymond Leblanc. Not only was Leblanc a Tintin fan – 'before the war I was a fervent reader of Tintin and Snowy's adventures in the *Vingtième Siècle*'[1]– but he was also an authentic resistance hero, who had spent the previous five years following the boy reporter's example. Leblanc was the kind of man who could obtain somebody a coveted 'certificate of good citizenship' without much trouble. Such trivialities as paper by the ton and ink by the gallon were as nothing to him. His brilliant idea was *Tintin* magazine, a new weekly that would re-create the golden days of the *Petit Vingtième*, only in full colour. There would be two pages of Tintin a week, drawn by Hergé. There would also be a job for Jacobs, and Jacques Van Melkebeke would be the editor.

It was not long before the optimism displayed by Haddock in Hergé's little self-parody turned very sour. In theory Leblanc's proposal was a deliverance. In practice, although he probably had no choice in the matter, it was not what Hergé wanted at all. True, the period between losing his job in September 1944 and receiving his certificate in May 1946 was a struggle, but in some respects it was also rewarding. All the Tintin books save *Cigars Of The Pharaoh* and *Tintin In The Land Of The Soviets* (which he wanted to forget) had been coloured. Also, the enemy he was facing during this period, if unyielding, was at least tangible. Prejudice, hysteria and ignorance were straightforward foes. *Tintin* magazine, on the other hand, represented a loss of Hergé's new-found independence. Two pages a week in colour was a very tall order, especially if he wished to maintain his escalating artistic standards: feeling insecure about money, he had let his agent work out the deal. He felt exploited, and did not enjoy life on the magazine. Yet because his employer was also his deliverer, he found it virtually impossible to protest without seeming ungrateful and mean-spirited.

Tintin magazine got off to a flying start on 29 September 1946, and was soon selling 100,000 copies a week in Belgium and Holland, with a French edition following two years later. Hergé carried on where he had left off with *The Seven Crystal Balls*, although he renamed it *The Temple Of The Sun (Prisoners Of The Sun* in English), as that had more relevance to the second half of the story. Almost immediately, however, things started to go wrong. The persecutors of Jacques Van Melkebeke rearrested him for having worked during the war, and this time he was sentenced to several months in jail. He had to resign as editor.

Then came the big bust-up with Jacobs. Hergé was having trouble coping with the demands of two full pages a week – *Prisoners Of The Sun* is a colourful story – not to mention other considerations such as pacing the plot of the whole story while ensuring that each episode ended on a cliffhanger. Jacobs demanded equal billing in return for his help. In future it would be 'Hergé And Jacobs' Adventures Of Tintin'. Hergé refused, and the partnership came to an end acrimoniously.

Jacobs had always considered himself very much Hergé's equal. When a journalist asked him how Hergé let him down if his work didn't come up to scratch, he replied, 'No problem. Hergé explained it quite simply, just as I did when he wanted my advice.'[2] Jacobs claimed to have thought of the title of *The Seven Crystal Balls*, which in fact probably derived from Hergé's promotional strip *The Crystal Ball*, the inspiration for Jo, Zette and Jocko. He also claimed to have thought up the secret tunnel into the Temple of the Sun, long before

Hergé drew it. Given the secret tunnel that helped Tintin find the forger's cave in *The Black Island*, this too could be taken with a pinch of salt.

Hergé was to work with Jacobs again, when the pair patched up their differences in later years, but only on a cash basis. Although they remained friends, Jacobs never worked on the plot of a Tintin story again. In fact it was the last time Hergé ever collaborated with anyone on an equal footing. In future, all his colleagues were to be employees, assistants who knew from the start who was boss; friendship would be a secondary consideration. In the short term he hired two young illustrators to help with his colouring work, Frank Jagueneau and Guy Dessicy, who is now the Director of the Brussels Cartoon Centre.

One would think that these troubles, and Hergé's dislike of the magazine, would manifest themselves in a lack of interest, and a slapdash approach. Quite the reverse. Hergé's work became more thorough, his dedication to detail more ferociously obsessive. The later stages of *Prisoners Of The Sun* are increasingly intricate, the composition of the frames more varied. Almost every frame is viewed from a different perspective, noticeably more so than in *The Seven Crystal Balls* or any of its predecessors. Tintin began to interfere with Hergé's home life, at least according to Germaine. That is to say, Tintin was interfering with Hergé's peace of mind, and his mood was affecting their marriage. At roughly the same time, his mother began to suffer her mental breakdown, which contributed further to his depression. His fortieth birthday probably didn't help either.

On 19 June 1947 the strain became too much, and Hergé disappeared. A notice appeared in *Tintin* magazine which read: 'Our friend Hergé is in need of a rest. Oh, don't worry, he's fine. But in refusing to marshal his forces to bring you a new episode of *The Temple Of The Sun* each week, our friend is a little over-worked.'[3] The tone of the notice was sarcastic to say the least. Hergé had vanished without any warning or explanation, and did not return for two months.

On his return, he continued to have difficulty with the amount of work he was expected to do. For instance, Leblanc had commissioned a mammoth collection of 'educational' illustrations, later issued as 5 inch × 8 inch picture cards, entitled 'Look and Learn'. The cards covered the entire history of transport, military and civil, on land, sea and air, and were launched by Tintin, Haddock and the pilot from *The Shooting Star*, retrospectively given the name of 'Major Wings'. Although all the boats, planes and so on were drawn by other artists, variously Jacobs, de Moor, Jacques Martin and Roger Leloup, Hergé himself had to draw literally hundreds of Tintin figures, each in a different costume. The fact that he was happy to draw Tintin in Nazi uniform where the wartime cards required it indicates a stubborn refusal to be dictated to by outside political interests, by atoning for a crime he felt he had not committed.

To enable Hergé to cope with his workload, a sizeable chunk of *Prisoners Of The Sun's* two-page spread was given over to a further educational series, a weekly blurb entitled 'Who Were The Incas?' This space-filler was apparently not enough. Early in 1948, Hergé disappeared again for six weeks, and another polite teeth-clenched notice appeared in the magazine. Leblanc demanded that other artists be brought in to carry the story forward in Hergé's absence. This forced Hergé back to work, but the suggestion made him blazing mad as well.

Bob de Moor: 'Leblanc was always unhappy with Hergé. All the other artists who drew for *Tintin* magazine – Jacobs, Martin and so on – they always began a new story the week after they ended the old one. But with Hergé, it was not the same. For all those years, forty years, there were always difficulties between Hergé and Leblanc. Despite which, the collaboration lasted many years. It was another kind of relationship with Casterman (who continued to publish the book versions). They were more understanding. Raymond Leblanc was more combative. Hergé said, "I can always count on Casterman." But I think with a man like Hergé, if it was not (a disagreement with) Raymond Leblanc, it was maybe another person.' Although he remained friendly and charming to those he had to work with, Hergé now chased up printers, distributors and other service departments, making sure their work met his increasingly perfectionist standards. Unavoidably, there were incidences of friction.

To Hergé's immense relief, *Prisoners Of The Sun* came to an end on 22 April 1948. It is rather surprising, after all the tribulations that accompanied the execution of the story, that the finished version is so good. One might have expected a high degree of technical expertise, after all the feverish toil that went into the artwork;

but the pacing, the retention of suspense right to the end, and the fine balance of humour and drama give no hint of the story's fragmentary origins.

Like *Red Rackham, Prisoners Of The Sun* is an epic journey conditioned by the suspense of not knowing what will happen at the end. Unlike *Rackham*, it successfully transfers the fear of its unknown adversaries from the first part of the adventure into the second. Tintin and Haddock travel to the heights of the Andes, to rescue the kidnapped Professor Calculus from an Inca funeral pyre. On the way Tintin befriends Zorrino, a native Indian boy who is being maltreated by white colonialist Europeans, in a throwback to his 1930s habits. Meanwhile the Thompsons undertake an extraordinary world tour, equipped with Calculus' pendulum, in their customarily doomed attempt to solve the crime.

It is Haddock, though, who provides the main source of the comedy once again. He is never far from humiliation at the hands of Peruvian wildlife, being licked by an anteater, charged by a tapir, tapped on the shoulder by a bear, eaten by mosquitoes and laughed at by monkeys. He gets a lizard stuffed down his back, sits on a passing crocodile in mistake for a log, and engages in a running battle with any llamas that happen to be passing.

Prisoners Of The Sun was originally drawn in *Tintin* magazine in a very curious format, horizontal instead of vertical, and three lines deep across two pages. This, together with the space-filling devices and sporadic interruptions, meant that when the story was finished Hergé had no idea whether or not it would fit the normal Casterman 62–page format. A considerable period of reworking followed, as a result of which it became clear that the adventure was far too long, and a number of sequences had to be cut.

Only one scene disappeared from the old *Le Soir* version of *The Seven Crystal Balls*, in the theatre, where Haddock laughs at the humiliation of audience members by the mind reader, and is himself humiliated by the revelation that his pocket is stuffed with spare monocles. The *Tintin* magazine half of the venture, by virtue of its more episodic structure, suffered far more. There were seven substantial cuts, as follows. Before Tintin's arrival on page 50 of what is now *The Seven Crystal Balls*, we see him on the bus with the same man who had been on the train at the very beginning of the whole adventure. Reading about the affair in a newspaper, Tintin then walks into a stream. Later, on line 4 of page 6 of what is now *Prisoners Of The Sun*, between frames 2 and 3, Tintin is almost captured on board the *Pachacamac* through his inability to get rid of the ship's black cat. On page 10, between frames 2 and 3 on the top line, when Haddock is trying to telephone the police at 4 a.m., he gets a Cutts-the-butcher style wrong number by mistake. On page 20, between frames 1 and 2 of the bottom line, Zorrino is captured by the Indians and manages to escape again. His rendezvous with Tintin and Haddock at the Bridge of the Inca is so surreptitious because the Inca are out looking for him. On page 22, between frames 2 and 3 of line 3, in a long sequence in the mountains, Haddock gets altitude sickness. Reviving himself whisky-fashion with coca-leaves, he roars up the track only to run into a skull balanced on a stick in his path. It is an Inca warning to go no further. On page 37, between lines 1 and 2, Haddock is attacked by a jaguar and by a poisonous snake, and saved by Tintin. In a scene which occurred between pages 44 and 47, now substantially reworked, the Captain finds several pieces of Inca gold lying about in the cave, and wastes precious time cramming his pockets with them. Then, when he and Tintin have to squeeze through a tiny hole in order to get any further, he reluctantly has to abandon the lot. One other Haddock joke was altered, in the last few frames of *The Seven Crystal Balls*: Nestor's complaint that his master has departed for Peru without any spare monocles originally referred to the fact that he had left without a single bottle of whisky.

In retrospect, one cut Hergé would have liked to have made was the ending. It reads ingeniously enough; Tintin saves his companions from death by appearing to command a solar eclipse he has read about in a newspaper, thus terrifying the natives and convincing Calculus that his execution is in fact a film shoot. In real life, though, the Incas were astronomers of some expertise. As worshippers of the sun they would have known all about a solar eclipse, a lapse in accuracy that always disturbed Hergé.

The rest of the book is accurate in every detail, as one would expect. Hergé used as his reference work a very old book, *Peru And Bolivia* by Charles Wiener, published in 1880. Wiener had explored the area in which Tintin and Haddock were journeying, and his painstaking record of the temples at Tiahuanaco and Sacsahuaman turned up in wholesale chunks in *Prisoners Of The Sun*. As well as geographic accuracy, Hergé wanted to make sure that his depiction of the human form was as lifelike as possible. Colleagues were forced to spend hours posing in striped ponchos while he sketched the folds of the cloth.

In 1969 the story was made into an animated-cinema film, together with *The Seven Crystal Balls*, collectively entitled *The Temple Of The Sun*. As with most screen versions of Tintin, Hergé had little artistic control over the film making, and the results depressed him. The plot was substantially altered to include the Thompson twins in the Andean section, while Tintin was armed with a sledge and tight jeans. The standards of artwork were far lower than those of the book. The wit, humour, suspense and accuracy that characterised the original had been emasculated.

Depressing as the results may have been, they were also commercially lucrative. Like the two *Rackham* books, the two Peruvian books have continued to be among the best selling and most popular Tintin stories. So much so that when (after a suitable interval) Hergé felt ready to continue with Tintin's career once again, he began his next adventure in exactly the same two-part pattern: first part to outline the mystery, second part to tell the story of the expedition. The results were to surpass all Hergé's expectations, becoming in the process the most famous of all the Tintin stories.

Hergé

Right: Hergé as a child with his younger brother, the inspiration for Tintin

Below: The young Georges Remi, still in the Boy Scouts at twenty (third from right)

Son papa le punissait tous les jours,

Il ne pensait qu'a jouer de bons tours.
Son papa le punissait tous les jours,
Mais cela ne servait jamais à rien,
Tintin recommençait le lendemain.

Maintenant que vous connaissez Martin,
Soyez bien gentil, donnez-moi la main
Et je vais vous conduire à la campagne
Où chaque année, en un coin de Champagne,
Tous les Simon vont passer les beaux jours
Chez un fermier, le père Kilabour.

Tintin-Lutin, a turn-of-the-century inspiration for Tintin

Neuvième année — N° 275.   Le Numéro : 40 centimes.   Dimanche 2 Mars 1919.

LE MIROIR

PUBLICATION HEBDOMADAIRE, 18, Rue d'Enghien, PARIS

LE MIROIR paie n'importe quel prix les documents photographiques d'un intérêt particulier.

L'AGRESSEUR DE M. CLEMENCEAU ARRIVE A LA SURETÉ APRÈS SON ARRESTATION

Le 19 février, au moment où M. Clemenceau venait de quitter en auto son domicile, rue Franklin, l'anarch
Cottin lui tira deux balles de revolver. Une des balles pénétra, par l'omoplate, entre les deux poum

The cover of *Le Miroir* from 1919 shows two dead ringers for the Thompson twins, who have just pulled off an arrest

Above: Henri de Donckers, as Tintin, Hergé and 'Snowy' emerge from Brussels' Gare du Nord at the end of Tintin's Russian adventure. The gentleman in the white pith helmet obscures the celebrated jar of hair grease

Right: Chang, at the time Hergé first met him

Above: Tintin and Adolf Hitler share the front page of the wartime *Le Soir*. Note the sub-editor's error in describing the two detectives as 'Durand & Durant'

Below: A crude wartime attack on Hergé in the anti-Nazi sheet *La Patrie*

Above: Hergé at home with his first wife, Germaine

Right: The original pre-Columbian fetish from Peru, complete with damaged ear, that Hergé used as a model for *The Broken Ear*

Above: Hergé with Fanny (far right) at the studios, at the time of *Tintin in Tibet*

Below: Leslie Lonsdale-Cooper, Hergé and Michael Turner in England in 1966. Turner's resemblance to Professor Calculus is, sadly, coincidental

19

Destination Moon

Objectif Lune

So tight was the production schedule at *Tintin* magazine, that Hergé had to begin work on his next adventure midway through *Prisoners Of The Sun*. As the first all-new Tintin story to begin since 1943, it had to be something special – and where could be more special than the moon? Six years later, when the story finally stumbled to a close, after further depressive interruptions and disagreements with Leblanc, it became clear that Hergé had created a technical masterpiece. No Hollywood-style bug-eyed monsters dressed up in bacofoil, but a depiction of lunar conditions that proved in due course to be uncannily accurate.

Ironically it was an obscure American science fiction film that provided the title of the story, making *Destination Moon* the only Tintin title to begin life in the English language; but Hergé's version of space was as far from the screen version as possible. He did his scientific research with a fanatical attention to detail that far outstripped any of his previous efforts. He built up a small library of astronomical works, and wrote to the author of *Man Amongst The Stars*, Dr Bernard Heuvelmans, to ask his advice.

Heuvelmans was delighted that the celebrated author of Tintin should turn to him for help, and came on board with a readiness bordering on rapacity. He didn't even wait for Hergé to start work on the moon adventure, joining in as technical adviser on the final eclipse scene of *Prisoners Of The Sun*. While Hergé brought his Peruvian adventure to a close, and prepared to complete his other bit of unfinished Tintin business, *Land Of Black Gold*, (which included, altogether, a further four months of unexplained absences), Heuvelmans and Jacques Van Melkebeke set to work on their own plot for *Destination Moon*.

Hergé had not enjoyed illustrating other people's ideas since *Flup, Nénesse, Pousette and Cochonnet* in the 1920s, and truth be told, he did not intend to start now. The Heuvelmans-Van Melkebeke plot was too silly to be compatible with his increasing realism anyway. It featured Professor Decimus Phostle from *The Shooting Star* as its main villain, who was prepared to sell the secrets of the moonrocket in order to pay for a diamond he wanted to give to the actress Rita Hayworth.

Hergé actually drew out the first two pages in black-and-white. The story was designed in the same horizontal format as the original *Prisoners Of The Sun*, and was set in America. It starts with Professor Calculus, in a radio interview, explaining that he wishes to visit the moon because it saved his life during the eclipse in Peru. As he speaks, barloads of Americans listening to the transmission laugh their heads off.

In the end, Hergé kept only two scenes from this plot, ingenious ideas arising from Heuvelmans' specialist knowledge of astronautics. Both involved Haddock: one, where Thomson inadvertently shuts off the artificial gravity of the spaceship with his walking stick, and Haddock's whisky floats off in a ball; the other, where the drunken Captain goes for a space walk and almost becomes a satellite of the asteroid Adonis. Both eventually found their way into *Explorers On The Moon*, on pages 5 and 8 respectively.

Hergé decided fairly swiftly that he did not like the Melkebeke–Heuvelmans storyline, nor the American setting, nor the format. The one concrete idea he did have – Tintin stuck in a snowdrift on the moon – was another disturbing and apparently meaningless recurrence of the colour white. *Tintin* magazine and its deadlines were getting on top of him once more. Hergé took off and mysteriously disappeared once again, and this time it was bad.

First, he went to Père Gall's monastery with his friend Marcel Dehaye, and sat in the grounds in a Red Indian tent for several weeks, reliving the old boy scout escape from the repressive order of his youth. His next destination was even more significant, indicative of a pilgrimage to revisit the turning points of his life, perhaps in search of reaffirmation that he had taken the right path. Hergé now made his way to Switzerland, and visited the Belgian King.

Since the war Léopold III had gone through similar dilemmas to Hergé, albeit on a grander scale. Having chosen to stay with his country in 1940, he had been imprisoned by the Germans; yet his personal intervention with Hitler is credited as having saved half a million Belgian women and children from deportation and forced labour. He could have fled, and joined the government in exile. Instead his attempts to retain neutrality and dignity had led to the bitterest punishment of all at the liberation, when he was driven from the country he loved. He and Hergé knew the pain of social ostracism. Both, perhaps, wanted to be reassured that they had taken the right decisions.

Hergé and the King struck up a friendship, and went fishing together on Lake Léman. It was an idyllic existence, and Hergé did not want to return. Wild notions entered his head of abandoning Tintin altogether – the trickle of book royalties had become a flood after the war, more than enough to support him in his own Swiss exile. Nemesis, however, was waiting back at his hotel. Letters from Leblanc, who was perhaps justifiably losing his patience, reminding him about his contract. Letters, too, from Germaine. If he would not return for her sake, would he not return home for the sake of Tintin?

After Hergé's marriage finally disintegrated a few years later, Germaine gradually disappeared from view, especially after Hergé's death. Official biographers now contend that she stifled his creativity and held him back. In fact the Abbé's former secretary, although plain and bourgeoise in the Belgian Catholic sense, was far from stupid. She had contributed children's stories to the *Petit Vingtième* herself, under the name of 'Tantine'. According to Bob de Moor, who knew them both well, she was a very active, determined woman with a sense of humour, whose organisational skills had proved useful to Hergé's early career.

In many respects, Germaine had been a substitute for Hergé's mother, with whom his relationship had been strained on account of her mental instability. 'Germaine was very much the maternal type, very solid, very nice,' recalls Leslie Lonsdale-Cooper. 'She was in his shadow, looking after him, carrying his coat and scarf, making sure he'd got everything. She was very much Georges' wife, in the background but taking care of him.' Now he was stubbornly outgrowing the need to be mothered.

Germaine's main failing was that she couldn't understand why a mere comic strip should have such an effect on her husband. She couldn't see how much Tintin had come to represent in his life; how the moral support she had always given him was no substitute for comprehension at this critical time. She resorted to the companionship of Madame Jagueneau, the mother of Hergé's temporary assistant Frank. Madame Jagueneau regarded herself as a faith-healer and mystic, capable of analysing Hergé's problems in terms of evil spirits and suchlike. It was the kind of illogical approach guaranteed to antagonise rather than conciliate Germaine's relatively rationalist husband.

On the professional side, a major disagreement was looming between Hergé and Leblanc over the matter of the commercial exploitation of Tintin. Leblanc was marketing Tintin purses, Tintin crayons, Tintin soap, Tintin writing paper, Tintin wallpaper, Tintin shirts,

Tintin caps, Tintin pennants, Tintin puzzles, and so on. By Leblanc's own admission, 'Hergé was clearly doubtful when I suggested trying such a scheme with his character.'[1] Furthermore, Hergé refused to draw advertisements that used Tintin to sell products. Said Leblanc, 'It fell to me to try and convince Hergé that factors other than his aesthetic criteria could dictate editorial decisions made by the company. Generally, I had to collect myself several times . . . Hergé showed a gradual disengagement from the magazine.'[2]

Hergé had worked out a rational solution to his difficulties. He would divorce himself as far as possible from what he saw as the exploitative tendencies of Leblanc, and go freelance once again. Not, this time, in solitary confinement at home, but in his own studios. He would resurrect the happy atmosphere of the *Petit Vingtième* in his own offices, where he would be boss once more. There he could work on *Destination Moon* relatively free from the pressures of the magazine, and he would hire a new collaborator to work on it. Not Heuvelmans, or Van Melkebeke, but a fresh mind for a completely new start. For a long time, no obvious candidates presented themselves. Hergé finished the *Land of Black Gold* alone. Ironically it was Leblanc himself who eventually provided the man Hergé needed: Bob de Moor.

'Hergé was sick yet again, and the director of the magazine, Leblanc, was very serious,' says de Moor. 'He told Hergé, "the only solution is to have somebody to help you".' Eugène Evany, who had worked on the *Petit Vingtième* with Hergé, recommended a junior on

Tintin magazine who had a similar style, who might be able to assist. 'People said my drawings when I was a beginner were like Hergé's, before I even knew Hergé,' de Moor explains. 'Not the same – Hergé was older, he was more experienced, he was a genius – but curiously there was a similarity.' Hergé wrote de Moor a letter offering him a short-term contract at the new studios, and the young artist accepted, little suspecting that he had just found his lifetime's work. Hergé had finally discovered the assistant he wanted; big, solid, reliable, talented, convivial and prepared to stick with him through thick and thin. 'Physically, he was Haddock without the beard – a good friend,' as Michael Turner put it. They never quarrelled once, in all their long association. The offer of work was, incidentally, the only letter Hergé ever sent to de Moor.

Bob joined up in 1951, early on in *Destination Moon*'s fragmentary history. Together the pair drew the whole of the two-part moon adventure unaided. Every background – every tiny star, every rock on every lunar mountain range, every spacesuit, every control panel and every rocket gantry, was drawn by Bob. Hergé drew in the figures and faces, composed each shot, worked on the story, and most audaciously of all, invented his own fully functioning nuclear spacecraft. (Although the astronomer Patrick Moore, called in as technical adviser on the British edition, found a flaw in the huge system that Belgian experts had missed.) The blueprint can be seen on page 35 of *Destination Moon*. It is based on the wartime V2 rocket, the nearest thing mankind had to space travel in 1951. Werner von

Braun, who had created the V2, eventually went to work on the US space programme, so NASA were obviously thinking along the same lines as Hergé.

Simply creating his own spacecraft was not enough. Hergé had to make sure it would work. He had a detailed scale model built by the hapless Heuvelmans, one that could be taken to pieces and inspected from every conceivable angle. Then he submitted it for approval to Professor Alexandre Ananoff, author of another book that had captured his imagination, entitled *Astronautics*. Every single frame of the finished work set inside the rocket was drawn from life, using the model as a background.

If anything, Hergé almost did too much research, or at least he was too proud of it. Usually he was happy that his research should sit happily in the background of a Tintin story. Indeed he considered it a virtue that it was all present and correct without interfering with the storyline. In *Destination Moon*, the Hergé theory of space travel is explained publicly from A to Z. It is hard going for younger readers, upsetting Hergé's normal balance of appealing to both adults and children without disturbing the other's enjoyment. The pill is sweetened, though, with some of the funniest sequences he ever wrote, featuring the deeply unscientific Haddock as fall guy. The invention of Calculus' goat fixation is a masterstroke, enabling the reader to tour the spacecraft in detail and in stitches, with Haddock in tow. The Professor's subsequent memory loss and Haddock's theatrical attempts to revive him are even better. Hergé's ability to be funny on paper seemed almost inversely proportionate to his enjoyment of life in general.

Some of Haddock's best moments come early on in the story, when he and Tintin first arrive in Syldavia. Perhaps because of his uneasy relationship with the USA, Hergé had decided on a European rocket launch from his imaginary Balkan republic. Before the war Borduria and Syldavia had represented Germany and its victims. Now they became symbolic of the east–west struggle, not unlike a sort of cold-war Bulgaria and Yugoslavia. King Ottokar of Syldavia had disappeared with the war, like his Yugoslavian counterpart; but the worst of the changes, at least as far as the whisky-loving Haddock was concerned, was that Syldavia had now established itself as the mineral water capital of the world.

The Syldavian–Bordurian enmity provided the villainy to keep a sense of danger running throughout *Destination Moon*. Mysterious glimpses of the saboteurs who intend to steal the moonrocket are drip-fed into the plot, in a manner Hergé had first used on *The Shooting Star*. It becomes clear that there is a traitor on the space centre staff, and in a vain attempt to entrap him Tintin gets shot. Five pages later he winds up in a hospital bed. There, leaving Tintin incapacitated, Hergé vanished again.

This time, Leblanc's notice in *Tintin* magazine was no longer acidly polite, but blunt and to the point. 'Hergé has disappeared.' Michael Turner explains: 'I don't think the commercial pressures were really hitting him until now. He was surrounded by all these people who were making money out of him. I think before that he was just a working artist.' Tintin was now very big business. Of course the boy reporter had always been a lucrative property, but to some extent Hergé had previously been shielded by his newspapers from the size, popularity and commercial vulnerability of his creation. Leading his own magazine from the front, he was far more exposed.

Throughout the interruptions, Bob de Moor continued to work away discreetly in the large house that contained the fledgling Studios Hergé. 'In the beginning, for five years, nobody knew that I was working with Hergé – only my friends and the editorship of *Tintin* magazine.' Hergé's principal vice appears to have been an unwillingness to share credit, although the fear of losing his independence was undoubtedly a contributory factor. In later, more confident years, it actually occurred to Hergé that Bob might be useful in taking some of this commercial heat off him. As well as imitating his style and therefore doing half his work, Bob could field the press, for instance, or the crowds of aspiring cartoonists seeking jobs. 'Years later, when Hergé was drawing fewer stories, he would say to me, "Oh you go and see the journalists, I am tired", or "I have no time".'

Hergé was certainly in need of Bob's skills when he tried to start work on *Destination Moon* once again. As soon as he tried to draw Tintin, Hergé's body refused to obey his unwilling mind. The skin on his hands split open in revolt. It was the first of many eczema attacks that were to become synonymous with drawing Tintin for the rest of Hergé's life. Somehow, through this debilitating pain, Hergé managed to plan out and illustrate the second part of the moon adventure, *Explorers On The Moon*. Born out of adversity, it is now regarded by many as his greatest artistic achievement.

20

Explorers On The Moon

On A Marché Sur La Lune

When Armstrong and Aldrin stepped out on to the surface of the moon from their Apollo spacecraft, all the world gasped. All, that is, except Tintin readers, who had already known for two decades that the moon looked like that. Technically, *Explorers On The Moon* is a work of genius, easily on a par with the likes of Jules Verne and H. G. Wells. Hergé made his living from his imagination, but he also knew when to rein it in. His uncannily accurate prediction of lunar conditions was a direct result of thorough study and the intelligent application of logic, with no room for the errors his imagination might have provided.

There are only two mistakes, and one of those is deliberate. Hergé had designed space helmets remarkably like the ones currently in use, but changed to a Perspex goldfish bowl type so that the characters could be identified more easily. The other inaccuracy – the existence of ice on the moon – came about at the insistence of Dr Bernard Heuvelmans. Hergé had agonised about the question, not at all sure if he agreed with prevalent scientific theory that the moon was an icy place, but Heuvelmans' advice won the day. At least it was to be twenty years or so before the mistake was confirmed.

What made Hergé's version of the moon – or to be more accurate, Bob de Moor's version of the moon as directed by Hergé – revolutionary for its time, was the absence of fashionable alien life. Hergé did allow himself one little joke on the subject, when the Thompsons discover what appear to be their own footsteps in the lunar dust, in the manner of their desert tomfoolery in *Land Of Black Gold*. That aside, his dull, dusty, arid lunar world was a brave creation, utterly vindicated by events.

Where his imagination did run riot was on board ship. The adjective 'surreal' is a hackneyed one to describe the sudden eruption of high-speed rainbow tufts of hair from the Thompsons' temples, but the contrast with the almost scholastic nature of the rest of the story is abrupt. The idea was a fairly recent one, stemming from the latter stages of *Land Of Black Gold* a few years back, and to some extent its inclusion indicates the increasing limitations of the Thompsons' uncomplicated stupidity in Hergé's changing world. To be fair, one rather fine scene featuring the twins did have to be cut for space reasons – it would have fitted in where the last frame on page 31 now sits. The detectives begin to run out of oxygen on their moonwalk, and are about to prise off their helmets to let in a little fresh air when Tintin intervenes. (Another short scene cut for space reasons involved Snowy almost being jettisoned with a bundle of the detectives' discarded hair.) Yet the moon adventure is the last time until *Tintin And The*

Picaros, more than twenty years later, that Thompson and Thomson accompany Tintin on an expedition. Haddock's presence obviated the need for other clumsy characters, reducing the detectives' role merely to that of spanners in the works. In future, they would generally stay at home.

From an artistic point of view, the episode of the Thompsons' rampant follicles deliberately injects a few bright splashes in a story otherwise notable for its carefully restrained colour scheme. For the first time, on the moon books, there is a sense of overall page design. Towards the end of *Destination Moon*, as if Hergé has suddenly realised that he is now free of newspaper restrictions, not to mention the bother of adapting cumbersome horizontal formats, he abandons the conventional four-line design of the Tintin stories with bravado. Whole pages – almost – are given over to stark, boldly composed illustrations. On page 13 of *Explorers On The Moon*, for instance, the moon is suddenly transformed by a violent increase in frame size from a little disc on an instrument panel into a huge and frightening planet. The red-and-white rocket plunging towards it, banal instructions issuing from its control cabin radio, is conversely reduced from an object of impressive size and solidity to a bright speck in a sea of black and brown.

Other pages opt for more intricate and complex designs, ground-breaking at the time, unified by shades of orange and brown. Pages 35, 36 and 37, for instance, all deal with the same trip into the icy lunar caverns of Heuvelmans' imagination, but the look and colour of each page is entirely different. When the nature of the Bordurian plot to take over the spacecraft is revealed in the second half of the book, the tension of the abortive take-off is heightened by quick cross-cutting between narrow horizontal frames of Jorgen and Wolff on their bunks.

The question of the villains' unusually sticky ends in *Explorers On The Moon* raised a flurry of moral indignation which proved that, to some extent, the attitudes of inter-war Belgium still held sway in 1953. Colonel Jorgen (he of the Rommel haircut, last encountered as the royal aide-de-camp in *King Ottokar's Sceptre*) blackmails the engineer Frank Wolff into helping him hijack the rocket. With the oxygen running out on the return journey, Wolff, racked by guilt, sacrifices himself to save the others, a gesture inspired by the celebrated Captain Oates. Suicide carried an enormous moral stigma in Catholic Belgium, and this was not acceptable on *Tintin* magazine. Hergé was forced to add an extra sentence to Wolff's farewell note that reads 'Perhaps by some miracle I shall escape too.' He always regretted inserting this line, which deflected the point of Wolff's action. 'Wolff was condemned, and he knew it better than anyone else,' said Hergé.

Perhaps in order to distance himself from this sort of ignorance, Hergé decided it was time to expand his studios. As the moon story drew to a close, he deliberately began to poach the better members of the *Tintin* magazine staff. Initially, there had been just three employees – Bob de Moor, Guy Dessicy the colourist, and Marcel Dehaye, the friend from the scouting trip to the monastery, who looked after secretarial duties. To this nucleus Hergé added Jacques Martin and Roger Leloup from Leblanc's 'Look and Learn' series, Jacobs (on occasion), Eugène Evany, and a lettering expert, Michel Demaret. A new secretary, a tall aristocratic type named Baudouin Van Den Branden, was also hired.

The practical effect of this expansion was to turn the process of creating a Tintin book into a veritable production line, the artwork passing back and forth from person to person, everyone knowing his part, like a little artistic orchestra with Hergé conducting. The underlying intent behind the changes, however, seems to have been to wrest control of the production process from Raymond Leblanc, and restore Hergé's independence. In the long term, the creation of Studios Hergé did succeed in polarising power away from Leblanc; what it did not do was make Hergé happy. In the end, the sheer weight of responsibility probably had the opposite effect. There were eighteen months of interruption on *Explorers On The Moon*.

In 1953, at least, Hergé felt strong enough to resist the commercial entreaties for a sequel to the moon books. In one of the funniest and most exciting endings to any Tintin story, Tintin & Co. arrive back at the Sprodj Rocket Base unconscious through lack of oxygen. The massed expertise of modern medical science is powerless to revive Haddock until someone mentions the word 'whisky'; whereupon the Captain springs from his stretcher and announces that he would rather be turned into a bollard than set foot in space again. Once again Hergé was putting his own words into the Captain's mouth. Despite the enormous pressure put on him to send Tintin to Mars or Jupiter, Hergé felt he had stretched reality more than enough already. (Ironically, and to Hergé's great amusement, a small dwarf planet between Mars and Jupiter – similar to Adonis – was actually named after him in 1982.)

He also felt strong enough to resist pressure of a different kind, when he was asked to change the title of the second part of the story. *They Walked On The Moon*, as *Explorers On The Moon* is known in the original French, was considered a little too matter-of-fact for such a dramatic tale. When pressed to change it, Hergé threatened *No Salami For Célimène* as the only possible alternative, and that was the last he heard of the matter. No more than witty bloody-mindedness perhaps, but it was the start of a coherent resistance that even if it did not banish Hergé's depressive spells, at least went hand-in-hand with them. After three successive double-length adventures, all enormously popular variations on the exploration theme, his publishers and magazine editors wanted nothing more than another such adventure. Instead, Hergé decided to jump the other way. He had not dared start an overtly political story since before the war. The possibilities of the new cold war-style Syldavia and Borduria that had been raised in *Destination Moon* excited him. He would be contrary, for the time being at any rate. His new multi-faceted production process would be turned on no less a target than the superpower struggle for control of the nuclear bomb.

21

The Calculus Affair

L'Affaire Tournesol

By the start of *The Calculus Affair* the Tintin factory was in full swing, every page the combined effort of several artists. The results were magnificent. 'There are many people who think Hergé said to his people "You do this", "you do that",' explains Bob de Moor. 'No, everybody was drawing, Hergé too. The page was going from Martin to Leloup to Michel Demaret, from one man to another, and then back to Hergé.' Often there would be as many as ten or twenty alternative versions of each page. Not only had the overall look to be appealing, but the reader had to be kept in suspense every time he flipped over a page, each frame had to be exactly the right size for the drawing it contained, and all without disturbing the pace and flow of the plot. Hergé said, 'If I reach page 42 and I think of a better idea for page 15, then I have to start all over again from page 15.'

Hergé's precision was by now more or less fanatical. He changed his working methods in two fundamental ways, in order to achieve a greater degree of realism. First, he abandoned his old system of drawing each page in pencil, then inking it in. Instead, scores of marginally different pencilled possibilities were drawn on the same page, before the best one was chosen and traced on to a separate sheet. This process could be repeated over and over again.

Every figure, every object and every landscape depicted in this way were to be drawn from life, to eliminate the slightest vestige of unreality. Every location in *The Calculus Affair* is taken from the real world; Hergé travelled to Switzerland with a camera and sketchbook to record Geneva's Cointrin Airport, Cornavin Station and Cornavin Hotel (page 17), Professor Topolino's house at Nyon (page 22) and the road through Cervens (pages 33–40). For the sequence in which Bordurian spies force Tintin's cab off the road and into Lake Geneva, Hergé scoured the selfsame road until he found a corner at Trevon where a car could actually do that.

He himself modelled the poses he wished his characters to take up, standing for hours in the studios while his artists sketched him, taking careful note of the way his clothes creased with each move. The angle at which he stood was a vital component in the second new technique Hergé brought to bear on his production process; the conscious use of filmic techniques to compose his narrative. Michael Turner: 'It's something that he mentioned on several occasions. I was very interested in the way that he would plot a room beforehand. From about 1954 the rooms suddenly became real. He explained that from then on, every setting was conceived as a film set; people moved in real rooms in a three-dimensional sense. He also said he worked very closely to long-shot, mid-shot and close-up, and that he consciously varied the use of a particular view. He felt he was his own film director in that way.'

Hergé had moved as far away as possible from the surface jollity of his early 1930s drawings. He had also lost the personal jollity that went into his early work; but in compensation for the loss of spontaneity, his technique had immeasurably improved. His principal artistic aim, as he later outlined it in a letter to Chang, was now better served than ever. 'My most important objective has always been . . . to make sure that my drawings are clear and legible, in such a way that at any part of the story the reader can immediately tell who is who and what is what.'[1]

If Hergé had eliminated the imagination from his representations of people and places, he had replaced it with a far more imaginative composition, design and visual wit. Where he did divert from the photographically accurate, in the faces of his characters, he had become a masterful caricaturist, capable of encapsulating entire moods in a tiny line or two. One has only to observe Captain Haddock trying to be polite to Jolyon Wagg to see the truth of this.

If these changes could be described as tactical successes, then strategically, too, Hergé had plans. He was very interested in Walt Disney's techniques, and was not averse to the idea that his studios might one day mount a European challenge to the Disney organisation. 'He was very conscious of what Disney did,' says Turner. It is difficult not to speculate that a degree of rivalry with Raymond Leblanc was also involved.

As one who had long detested authority, especially of the bureaucratic sort, Hergé intended his studios to be a sort of artistic kibbutz, with everyone free to work on their own projects as well; but like Disney, he soon found there was no substitute for personal direction. 'A clear chain of command', as he put it. In fact he became something of a sergeant-major at work. The Studios Hergé was not the sort of place where you turned up late in the morning, or nipped out for a quick coffee without permission. It was scrupulously clean and tidy for an artists' studio, and even more revealingly, all the desks faced the same way. With Hergé playing the martinet in the pursuit of perfection, one would think that the artists brought in to work on *The Calculus Affair* would have begun to show signs of disaffection. Not a bit of it. The staff regarded him with loyalty and affection bordering on hero-worship. His ability, record of achievement and immense personal dignity led to his being held in almost godlike esteem.

Of course this must in part have been due to the new employees' youth and inexperience, faced with Hergé's immense and still growing reputation. He was hardly treated with such respect at home. One member of staff he did fall out with was his old friend Jacques Van Melkebeke, who like Jacobs seemed unable to come to terms with Hergé's increasingly massive success. He carped about his new employer behind his back, leading to a huge row. Ironically, Van Melkebeke had just brought him a prospective plot synopsis for a Tintin adventure set in Tibet, an idea which Hergé promptly tore up as unworkable, causing Van Melkebeke to walk out.

This was, however, an isolated blast. For the most part the studios seemed to flourish under Hergé's benevolent dictatorship, turning out all the Tintin advertising commissions and greetings card illustrations that he wasn't especially keen to knuckle down to. The long-awaited revising and colouring of *Cigars Of The Pharaoh* got underway too. The rest of the time was spent working on *The Calculus Affair*, as Hergé raced to get each weekly episode completed for *Tintin* magazine. No witnesses now exist to the creation of any of the pre-war or wartime stories; all of the old guard are dead – Wallez, Jacobs, Van Melkebeke, and of course Hergé himself. With the arrival of Bob de Moor and the others, however, we are suddenly privy to a number of eye-witness accounts, enabling us to assess the sort of man Hergé had become.

That he was keen to get every detail right is clear, but he was not, insists Bob de Moor, obsessive. 'Hergé was exacting in his work, without being obsessive. He was a man we admired very much – we were the obsessive ones. I remember once that the *back* of a strip showed traces of pencil; I rubbed them out and *he* found that a little excessive. Against that, he advised me, "when you draw vegetation, you must draw it inside five minutes. Then go back over it several times, when it is possible to give it more depth and authenticity".'[2]

Hergé's meticulous nature had its generous side. He personally replied to every fan letter sent to him, and wrote positively, encouragingly and at length to even the most hopeless of aspiring illustrators. He gave away valuable drawings to his fans. He did find sociability an effort though, and hated meeting the press or public in person. There was a reserved, unostentatious side to his character instilled in him by his upbringing, so these painful duties usually devolved on Bob de Moor or Jacques Martin.

Martin was Hergé's other main assistant, a short, dark, jolly Gallic type who shared de Moor's high regard for his boss and his ability to ape the Hergé style. 'Jacques' work is in some ways closer to Hergé's than any of the others in his manipulation of line,' says Michael Turner. Besides intelligence and gentility, Martin identified Hergé's great reserve of patience as his chief quality, a patience that had developed as a reaction to a quarter of a century of being cajoled and hurried by editors to get his artwork done on time. When Martin passed him some work demanding a quick reply, Hergé put it in a drawer saying, 'In six weeks this will seem less urgent.'[3] Time didn't matter, only the result. This was not procrastination, but a precise and independent attitude.

If he had a fault, according to Martin, it was egocentricity, but of the self-confident rather than the arrogant kind. This was also the opinion of Roger Leloup, the transport specialist who drew the tank sequence in *The Calculus Affair*. 'Hergé was very egocentric,' said Leloup. 'He lived only for the world of Tintin and within the limits of its success. I don't blame him,'[4] he added. Hergé was quick to confirm this. 'I'm a dreadful egotist. I draw for the child I was and still am. If Jacques Martin or Bob de Moor has a good idea, I convince myself completely and forever that it was mine.' Hergé rarely argued with anybody, but when he did he never conceded the argument. Usually, he turned arguments into a joke – he was capable of turning anything into a joke – but he never gave in.

Certainly, he was a very funny man, whose wit was always slightly suppressed in real life, although it appears to have been captured in his work. Even in his blackest moments he was capable of self-deprecating humour. People, especially, made him laugh, but never out loud. Curiously, for one so quick-witted and amusing, Hergé was extremely vulnerable to the practical joke. At the Studios Hergé there appear to have been many of these, often directed at his particular neuroses. Once, he returned from holiday to find the studio massively untidy, strewn with empty bottles, dirty washing and other evidence of debauchery. Another time – a joke that didn't go down so well – a Tintin page was drawn without his permission. His fear of commercial exploit- ation was lampooned when his staff managed to persuade him that a new range of Tintin potties was being manufactured, without his permission, with Tintin's face looking up from the inside saying, 'I can see you, you little rascal.' He went wild. On a more trivial level, his ambivalence towards opera also pro- vided the staff with a joke at his expense. He was informed that the famous singer Liliane Harvey, on a tour of Brussels, had requested an audience with him. With some trepidation, he agreed. 'Liliane Harvey' turned out to be Bob in a dress.

Away from these well-documented studio larks, Hergé was an intensely private individual, and there is almost no record of his home life. His hobbies, such as they were, seem to have been art collecting, gardening, wine, jazz, Eastern philosophy and looking after cats, although most enjoyable of all was simply doing nothing. He found Tintin exhausting, and tended to divide his time between working on his current story and recharging his batteries, 'Time spent lazing around is not time lost,' he insisted. His secretary Baudouin Van Den Branden always maintained that it was important to distinguish between the vigorously hard-working Hergé and the lazy Georges Remi. He was famous enough by now to have become something of a recluse. Success had brought good food and wine and clothes. It had also brought with it the unwelcome attentions of the medi-ocre, a class of people with which Belgium seems to have been well stocked. Hergé could be incredibly polite and courteous to such people, in a patrician sort of way that belied his suburban origins. Deep down he detested mediocrity more than anything else. 'The only thing I would censor is mediocrity,' he confessed, 'but who would be the judge of it?' In fact Hergé violently objected to censorship of any sort, an interesting view for one whose stories were so moral, suggesting a high level of self-censorship. A conflict is apparent here. Obviously, on one level, he had reasoned his way out of his childhood Catholic morality. Certainly, he had abandoned religion per se. On another level, his own personal morality had not escaped the constrictions of childhood. In as far as he felt himself optimistic by reason and pessimistic by nature, Hergé too recognised this division.

Fortunately for Tintin readers, Hergé's detestation of

mediocrity manifested itself in one of his finest characters, Jolyon Wagg. Wagg was intended as a vicious satire on Belgian bourgeois vulgarity, but his type is instantly recognisable the world over. It is surprising that Wagg took so long to arrive, given Hergé's fascination with his kind. He was actually based on someone Hergé met during the war, who strolled into his home, pointed at a chair and asked its owner to 'have a seat'. 'He's the sort of person who's completely satisfied with himself,' explained Hergé, 'not a wicked man, but very smug.'

Wagg's dramatic entrance into the early stages of *The Calculus Affair* follows the pattern set by Hergé's wartime visitor fairly closely. In the middle of a violent thunderstorm, glass is inexplicably shattering all around Marlinspike, and mysterious strangers are firing revolvers in the grounds. Wagg breezes in uninvited as if it were a motor rally. 'Nice little place you've got here. Must say I prefer something more modern, but still . . . is that whisky you're drinking? You can pour one for me while you're about it. Not that I like the stuff; I'm just thirsty, that's all. Not bad armchairs, these. I don't stand on ceremony, you know. A bit of a clown. That's me. Never a dull moment with me around, you bet.' All of us have at some time or other encountered the Wagg type.

In French the character is known as Seraphin Lampion, the surname meaning a chintzy little lamp of the sort Wagg would use to decorate his home. At one stage Hergé was going to call him 'Crampon', but thought the name too hard-sounding. Of all the names in the English editions of Tintin, none received a more perfect translation than Jolyon Wagg of the Rock Bottom Insurance Co. He is the kind of person, explained Hergé, who wears a belt and braces at the same time. The kind you meet by the hundred on foreign beaches where you have travelled to avoid them.

By 1954, Hergé was well into his Haddock persona, and used Wagg's visits to torment himself vicariously. Wagg turns up in every Tintin book hereafter, bar the exceptional *Tintin In Tibet*, and most of the episodes in which he features are based on real frustrations from Hergé's life. Endlessly complacent, breezily insensitive, Wagg's every appearance was like a self-inflicted dentist's drill to Hergé. 'I myself find his habit of always telling stories about his Uncle Anatole very irritating.'

Rooted less in fantasy and more in the real post-war world than its immediate predecessors, *The Calculus Affair* introduced other memorable characters besides Wagg. The long run of double-length adventures had relied upon character comedy, but of a type that derived from the interrelation of familiar characters in an alien setting. *The Calculus Affair* returned to the *King Ottokar's Sceptre* range of political, national and domestic types as a source of caricature. Fifteen years on, the humour was more sophisticated than before.

On the domestic front, there is Cutts the butcher, the perpetual wrong number, who resides at Marlinspike 431 (not 421). Internationally, there is a plethora of cold-war Syldavian and Bordurian agents, the former distinguished by their luxuriant moustaches, the latter by their shaven heads and abysmal telephone system.

Best of all is Colonel Sponsz, another Brussels slang word meaning 'sponge', the stiff-necked chief of the Bordurian secret police. Sponsz was an evil caricature of Hergé's brother Paul, whom he still did not get on with very well. The militaristic Paul had been the model for Tintin all those years before. Now the celebrated quiff had been isolated, with age, by a receding tide of hair, forming a ridiculous little island in the middle of his forehead. As a young soldier Paul had suffered tremendous ribbing as 'Major Tintin', and had adopted an Erich von Stroheim image as a diversion. Not to be defeated, Hergé now ruined his life all over again. Satirists who really want to know what Tintin would look like as a middle-aged man have only to look at Colonel Sponsz.

Sponsz is charged in *The Calculus Affair* with the security of Professor Calculus, who has been kidnapped and taken to Borduria. Like the Syldavians, the Bordurians are after the secret of his latest invention, a form of sonic weapon that can destroy glass and porcelain. Recognising that, with a little tweaking, the machine should be able to destroy not only china but China, agents of both countries involve the Professor in a violent tug-of-war, unaware like everyone else that the plans are actually sitting on his bedside table at Marlinspike all along.

In the well-researched tradition of all the post-war Tintin books, the sonic weapon had a factual basis, being an abortive German experiment from the Second World War. In *The Calculus Affair*, however, it is elevated to the status of ultimate weapon, a doomsday machine which could conceivably destroy the world. With the Soviets' development of the atom bomb in 1953, the nuclear threat dominated the news, and this was Hergé's contribution to the cold war debate. If it is not the most impassioned of his political satires, it is undoubtedly the most witty and sophisticated. The depiction of communist Borduria and its pretensions is perfectly observed, except that the Bordurian regime is not strictly communist but 'Taschist'. Statues of the nation's Stalin figure, Marshal Kûrvi-Tasch, dominate the city of Szohôd. His celebrated moustache can be found in miniature on the hotel lamp fittings, decorating Sponsz's uniform, on the grilles of cars, over the gate of the fortress of Bakhine, even as an accent in the Bordurian language.

The Swiss section of the story is no less beautifully observed. Tintin had been on sale in Switzerland since 1932, in a publication called *The Illustrated Echo*. Despite the yodelling implications of that title, Hergé wanted to draw a Swiss adventure free of national clichés to please his readers there. Some of the comic set pieces he offered them are his best ever. Haddock's futile attempts to rid himself of the sticking plaster from his nose, for instance (it turns up again in *Flight 714*, stuck to his right elbow on page 34); or the unforgettable car ride through Cervens with Arturo Benedetto Giovanni Giuseppe Pietro Archangelo Alfredo Cartoffoli da Milano; or the scene where Tintin and Haddock are flying over Lake Geneva in a helicopter, being shot at by Syldavians, and the only person they can raise on the emergency radio frequency is a disbelieving Wagg, transmitting on his ham radio set. 'Ha! ha! ha! you old humbug, you! But you can't catch Jolyon Wagg that easy! You can't teach your grandmother to suck eggs, you know! By the way, what about your insurance?'

On the basis of these elements alone, *The Calculus Affair* is probably the best of all the Tintin books. Unfortunately it suffers from a structural fault, in that the ending is rushed and slightly unsatisfactory. It was the first single-volume adventure Hergé had started since 1941. Also, for some inexplicable reason, the final sequence of the magazine version reverted briefly to the old horizontal format from *Prisoners Of The Sun*. When it was converted to the vertical for the book edition, a number of frames had to be lost, spoiling the pacing somewhat in the book's last few pages.

After escaping by tank from Borduria thanks to the convenient incompetence of the local artillery, Tintin, Haddock and Calculus rush back to Marlinspike, where the Professor discovers his microfilm and promptly destroys it to save mankind from certain doom. In anyone else's hands, this could have been a mawkish scene. Who else but Hergé would have Calculus inadvertently set fire to the Captain's beard in the process? *The Calculus Affair* had been a triumph, vindicating Hergé's decision to abandon the double-volume expedition format, and to change his working methods.

Yet the creation of the studio system, intended to take the commercial and artistic heat off him, had merely had the reverse effect, by adding to the weight of responsibility that Tintin represented. Hergé's sporadic absences and stoppages through eczema continued unabated. Despite the fact that he was now creating his best work, he was doing it in defiance of his own unhappiness. He would have liked to have thrown in the towel and given up altogether, but that would have represented a defeat. 'The cartoons all started as fun,' he said. 'Then they became a job. Now I feel I have to take care because of their importance to children.'[5]

'As the years went by,' says Bob de Moor, 'he was very pleased that I could be there at the studio (in his absence). Now and then he had the courage to start work again. He said, "I am responsible, as the studio head." The studio for him was something depressing. He would say, "I have to come back, there are people there waiting for me".' Faced with these interruptions, the patience of his staff must have matched Hergé's own. Obviously his personal and professional lives were converging towards a major crisis. There was nothing he could do now but let it happen.

22

The Red Sea Sharks

Coke En Stock

Throughout this increasingly desperate period in Hergé's life, few signs of the turmoil he was going through intruded into the Tintin books, which were now selling a million copies a year. He was now working twenty-five to thirty weeks ahead of *Tintin* magazine, as a buffer against his impromptu absences. The only signs of the malaise afflicting him were a few wry jokes at his own expense here and there, and the sporadic torture of Haddock by a cast of characters straight out of his own nightmares. It was to be one more book before his personal life suddenly irrupted into Tintin's with a vengeance; but coming just before the crisis, *The Red Sea Sharks* is a story unusually full of the type of people Captain Haddock liked to avoid. Not just Wagg, but Bianca Castafiore and Abdullah too are on hand to make Haddock's life a misery. Captain Allan, now linked up with Rastapopoulos, is cruellest of all, posing the fundamental question, 'Do you sleep with your beard under or over the sheet?', thereby ensuring Haddock a sleepless night of trial and error.

There are so many familiar faces floating around that *The Red Sea Sharks* has something of the flavour of a Tintin family reunion, the first of many. By 1956 Hergé's cast of characters had reached a size where he could derive humour simply by trying out new combinations of old favourites, poor Nestor's torture at the hands of Abdullah being a case in point. This self-referential element set a firm precedent for later books.

Dawson, Chief of the Shanghai Police from *The Blue Lotus*, pops up selling planes to General Alcazar, who is now more stand-offish than ever. The story actually starts with Alcazar, who is introduced rather ingeniously as Tintin and Haddock emerge from a cinema. Haddock is complaining about the film's plot: 'The end was too improbable. The old uncle hasn't seen his nephew for twenty years . . . he starts thinking about him . . . the door opens, and hey presto, who's there? The nephew! For example, take General Alcazar, whom you mentioned just now. He completely vanished from our lives years ago. Well, d'you suppose, if I just think about him he'll pop up on the street corner, like that, bingo!?' Cue a bone-crunching collision with Alcazar, coming around the next corner.

Another unexpected combination involves Sheikh Bab El Ehr, who has seized power in Khemed, and Dr Müller, now in his employ. Müller has taken on his third alias of the series, that of Mull Pasha – a clear reference to Glubb Pasha, the idiosyncratic British commander of the Arab legion who operated out of Jordan during the Second World War. As one would expect with an adventure set in Khemed, Sheikh Ben Kalish

Ezab and Oliveira da Figueira are there too, making *The Red Sea Sharks* almost a sequel to *Land of Black Gold*.

In a sense, *The Red Sea Sharks* atoned for the relative failure of the earlier book, the satirical thrust of which had been dissipated by events. The new story was based entirely on facts, and rather grim ones at that. Hergé had read a newspaper exposé confirming that slavery still existed, even as late as 1956. An Arab airline ferrying black African pilgrims to Mecca was diverting its planes and selling its customers as slaves. Hergé fictionalised the airline as 'Arabair', holder of the Khemed-to-Mecca concession. Tintin and Haddock are drawn into the conspiracy inadvertently when Alcazar drops his wallet at their street corner meeting, leading to a complicated exposure of Arabair's skulduggery that makes *The Red Sea Sharks* one of Hergé's more adult-orientated adventures. The code word for the slaves is 'coke'; hence the original French title of the book, *Coke En Stock*.

For the construction of the story Hergé retreated somewhat from using the full battery of studio staff, preferring to do the bulk of the work with Bob de Moor, although Leloup drew all the planes, cars and other machinery. Together they developed the plot using the bones of the newspaper story, working out a sequence here and there, before trying to fit the whole together as a jigsaw. They researched the long sequence on the freighter *Ramona* with a drunken trip on the MS *Reine Astrid*, a Swedish cargo ship running between Antwerp and Gothenburg. They also worked out the geography of Khemed, which emerged as a small state on the north-east side of the Red Sea, up the coast from

Mecca, and noticeably closer to Jordan than to any of the Gulf states it had resembled in 1939. The Emir Ben Kalish Ezab's Roman rock palace in the Jebel was taken directly from Petra in Jordan, and the long gulf out into the Red Sea, through which Tintin and Haddock travel by Sambuk, appears to have been based on the Gulf of Aqaba.

The Red Sea provided the climax of the story, when the good guys and bad guys finally stop skirting each other and come to grips. Captain Haddock steers the *Ramona*, brilliantly and accidentally by turns, in a gripping sea duel with a submarine. Tintin and he have rescued the ship's cargo of slaves, helped by the book's only new character, the likeable Estonian pilot Skut (originally Szut) who later pops up in *Flight 714*. They have only to dodge the torpedoes until they can be rescued by the seventh cavalry in the shape of the USS *Los Angeles*. These lantern-jawed US sailors are the first genuinely wholesome Americans to appear in a Tintin story, a change of direction not unconnected to the fact that negotiations were now underway with the Golden Press for Tintin books to go on sale in the USA for the first time.

It is a pity that in the excitement of the ending, Hergé abandons many of his loose ends. *The Red Sea Sharks* shares with *The Calculus Affair* the structural weakness of a rather hasty finish. 'In his prime period, Hergé was always overrunning,' recounts Michael Turner. 'Casterman, who were exploiting the books at 62 pages, were calling the tune, so he frequently had to scramble to a conclusion.' Even if Hergé had to use a page full of newspaper cuttings to resolve as many plot strands as possible, he had shown none the less that he could write a first-rate thriller. Also, in saving a boatload of Africans from slavery, he felt that Tintin had made up for *Tintin In The Congo*.

Others did not see it that way. The magazine *Jeune Afrique* heavily criticised *The Red Sea Sharks* for racism, and others joined the attack. Ostensibly, the African accents he had given the African characters were at fault, but in fact the scores were much older, dating back to the Congo. Hergé acknowledged that the earlier book might have merited the accusation, but *The Red Sea Sharks*, he protested, was completely innocent. Were not the villains all white men or Arabs? The anti-Hergé lobby agreed that this was the case and pondered the matter, before finally announcing that the book must therefore be racist towards Arabs. Hergé was sufficiently stung by the criticism to rewrite the Africans' dialogue in 1967, in a style closer to that spoken by American blacks. At the same time he endowed the Emir of Khemed with more flowery speech patterns, as befitted a monarch not a million miles away from the Sandhurst-educated rulers of Jordan and Oman. These changes did not affect the English translation, which had been completed in 1960.

The race debate was the sort of tiresome issue that he felt he could do without in 1958, when the story came to an end. He was a weary man. 'Shall I never be left in peace?! In peace!!' wails Haddock. The answer is no, of course, as Wagg turns up to see him with a whole motor rally in tow (to 'liven things up for the old stick-in-the-mud'). The motor rallyists did in fact turn up at Hergé's home three or four times a year, always without a flicker of an invitation. They had put his house on their itinerary, and even included banal questions about the place in a quiz competition that they all had to fill out. Needless to say no hints, not even their appearance in *The Red Sea Sharks*, could persuade them that they were not welcome. 'How can you stop Wagg from ringing your doorbell,' pleaded Hergé, 'and asking idiotic questions like "what is the weight of your railings?"' There was no respite, it seemed, either at work or at home.

By now Hergé's home life was deteriorating both physically and emotionally. The tidiness that characterised his studio had deserted his house, and Germaine was drawing ever closer to her friend Bertje Jagueneau; a state of affairs that was to culminate one evening when Hergé came home to find the pair of them indulging in a magical incantation intended to restore his affections. He was furious, but then he didn't want his affection restored to Germaine. There was a new lady in his life.

'Fanny Vlaminck and her friend France Ferrari were both young artists, newly hired by the studio,' remembers Michael Turner. 'They were absolutely stunning – in a very French sense. Chic style, you know, wearing very simple, good clothes, and no wonder he fell for her.' Before he started up his studio, Germaine had been his chief helper. Now there was no need for her in his professional life. His father Alexis took over the administrative side of Tintin – he even knew all about Fanny – and Germaine was left in the cold.

To his colleagues Hergé was a genius. To Germaine, who for obvious reasons preferred not to talk about it,

'Hergé was someone whose progress offered me moments of happiness, someone whose advance also revealed flaws. He was a human being. That's all.'[1] Now, as an alternative to this down-to-earth attitude, an incredibly elegant, attractive girl half his age, who shared many of his interests and who regarded him as a genius, was offering her companionship. It was not long before their relationship became more than strictly professional.

The tidal wave of guilt this unleashed in the mind of someone brought up in turn-of-the-century Belgium is difficult to appreciate. It was not long before Hergé had to tell his wife. Bob de Moor again: 'Hergé was a man of discipline and order. He confessed to his wife the first time. Another man would never say he was going with another woman, he would say nothing. Somebody else would tell the wife. No, with Hergé, he said, "I *have* to tell her." It was the boy scout in him – the man was like that. Maybe it wasn't a good way to handle it, that's his affair.' Life with Germaine was no longer possible.

Torn between loyalty to a long-standing relationship, and the potential release offered by the new liaison, Hergé began to experience white dreams again. These white dreams were not merely troublesome, however. They were blinding white, screaming nightmares. It was tantamount to a medical emergency, that doctors could not cure. Only Tintin, it seemed, could face the problem.

23

Tintin In Tibet

Tintin Au Tibet

Hergé dreamed himself alone at home, the world covered in snow, with little children playing outside. He goes out to make snowballs to throw at the children, and they disappear. At once, his responsibilities feel lifted. Then, he notices a dark patch – a rock – in the snow. He approaches it, and finds a tunnel, which he enters. At first, the going is easy; but gradually, as he gets further along the tunnel, the ground begins to slope upwards, more and more steeply. Large rocks begin to block the way. He has to heave these obstacles to one side to continue. The incline gets steeper and steeper, the passage narrower, the obstacles more difficult, the going harder. Eventually, he finds himself climbing an iron ladder, up a narrow vertical chimney through the rock. At last, there is light above him, the light of a blinding white sky and a snowy landscape. As he tries to climb out of the crevasse, however, he finds that the rungs of the ladder have bent over to form iron bars, blocking his way and sealing him in. The bars holding him prisoner have taken the shape of a church window . . .

This is just one of many dreams that Hergé recorded over a year of nocturnal torment, on a nightly theme of 'the beauty and cruelty of white'. It must take a prize for ease of interpretation. Catholic morality, pure as the driven snow, still had him in its guilt-ridden grip. Yet for straightforwardness, this dream was as nothing compared to the one about a train plunging down a track, then suddenly derailing and crashing. A veritable Freudian textbook case, lesson one.

In fact it was to a pupil of Jung's, the Swiss psychoanalyst Ricklin, that Hergé took his most frightening nightmare for explanation in April 1959. He dreamed that he found himself in a white tower built from a series of ramps, with everything around him covered by dead leaves. Then, in a bright white alcove, a completely white skeleton would suddenly leap out and try to trap him – at which point everything about him would turn bright white. Ricklin saw that Hergé was driving himself on to disaster, both emotionally and professionally. Hergé must destroy 'the white demon of purity' immediately. 'I don't want to discourage you,' he said, 'but you will never finish your life's work. In your place, I would just stop working now.'

In some respects, this was what Hergé wanted to hear. He had already considered giving up Tintin for a career in abstract art. In other respects, following Ricklin's advice meant admitting defeat, which was anathema. 'It meant turning upside down all my values – what a shock!' said Hergé. 'This was a serious moral crisis: I was married, and I loved someone else; life seemed impossible with my wife, but on the other hand

I had this scout-like idea of giving my word for ever. It was a real catastrophe. I was completely torn up.'

Hergé chose not to follow Ricklin's advice, but to implement the scout motto instead: 'A scout smiles and sings through all his difficulties.' A little trite perhaps, but what he actually did was draw out his troubles through *Tintin In Tibet*, a book of overwhelming whiteness and purity. It was ironic, but not perhaps unpredictable, that faced with the moral dilemma posed by Ricklin, Hergé chose to keep his scout's word of honour to Tintin, but not to Germaine, whom he left soon afterwards.

He had already begun work on the Tibetan adventure before visiting Zurich for psychoanalysis, but only after much internal agonising about the choice of story. At first, clutching at the scouting/Red Indian ethic for comfort, he had wanted to take Tintin back to the USA for a re-run of the Indian sequences of *Tintin In America*, with oil found on an Indian reservation. This was rejected as backward-looking. He had held on to the past before and although it had been a comfort it had not ultimately solved anything. Anyway, his friendship with ex-King Léopold continued to provide a nostalgic emotional prop.

One feeling that came through strongly was the need to write a story with no villains, or guns, or violence. Hence the second abortive idea, a judicial mix-up erroneously incriminating Nestor in some misdeed, with Tintin fighting to clear the butler's name. Yet Hergé's fundamental need was to draw a white, snowy adventure, so idea three concerned a polar exploration party going down with a mysterious type of food poisoning, and sending out an SOS to Professor Calculus. This, too, had a flaw. The new adventure must be a solo voyage of redemption for Hergé. Calculus could not go. Nor, for that matter, could any of the great cast of characters used in *The Red Sea Sharks*, not even the Thompson twins, not even Wagg. Only Tintin and Haddock would be allowed on this trip.

Which is where Chang came in. Since going free-lance from the *Petit Vingtième* all those years before, Hergé had enjoyed Tintin less and less. He had never enjoyed drawing the strip so much as during the golden days of *The Blue Lotus*. It was a source of massive regret that Chang had passed out of his life, and he still hoped to make contact with his Chinese friend again one day. Throughout the difficult post-war years, of all the nostalgic emblems that Hergé held on to, his friendship with Chang was the strongest, taking on a significance probably out of all proportion to their original relationship. Unlike the Red Indians, Chang was not a backward-looking symbol. Hopefully, he would be part of Hergé's future. The bright white purity of Hergé's friendship with Chang would be used to exorcise and replace the whiteness of guilt.

The story he finally opted for involved Chang supposedly dying in an air crash. Echoing the lachrymose final scenes of *The Blue Lotus*, Tintin sheds a tear at the news (Chang is the only character Tintin ever cries for), before suddenly deciding that his friend is not dead after all. He must mount an expedition into the inhospitable snows of the Himalayas, to bring their friendship out alive and intact once again. It was the first time since the war that Hergé had drawn his own thoughts and aspirations through Tintin, although the unwilling Haddock is always on hand, a constant reminder of the other half of Hergé's personality.

The Tibetan setting for the air crash was obviously something of an embarrassment, as it had been Van Melkebeke's idea at the time of their falling out; but their differences were patched up now and the story went ahead. It was a major project, with the studio in full swing, and every last Tibetan detail researched to the full. All the costumes are absolutely accurate, researched and drawn by Jacques Martin. Even the Indian Airways flight that crashed was chosen and depicted carefully, until Indian Airways got cross and ownership had to be credited to the fictitious 'Sari-Airways'.

One unexpected Tibetan detail that Hergé incorporated into the story was the Yeti, the mythical Abominable Snowman. Hergé chose to depict him as a remarkably unabominable type, a charming coconut-headed giant who rescues Chang from the aftermath of the crash. This was Heuvelmans' doing, who had contributed to the equally unclichéd approach to the moon. He had written another book, entitled *On The Tracks Of Unknown Animals*, containing a substantial section about the Yeti. Using this as a foundation, Hergé made it his business to investigate every sighting of the Yeti and its tracks. He interviewed mountaineers, including Maurice Herzog, who had spotted the tracks of an enormous biped which stopped at the foot of a sheer rock

face on Annapurna. Even the way in which the creature
cares for the starving Chang is taken from a sherpa's
account of a Yeti which rescued a little girl in similar
circumstances. If anyone does ever find a Yeti, you can
bet it will look something like Hergé's depiction of the
beast in *Tintin In Tibet*. If *The Red Sea Sharks* had atoned
for the race element in *Tintin In The Congo*, then the
Yeti in *Tintin In Tibet* did the same for Tintin's slaughter
of African wildlife.

The intensely personal nature of the story made this
Hergé's favourite Tintin adventure, supplanting *The
Secret Of The Unicorn* in his affections. The title is a clue
– aside from *Land of Black Gold*,[1] it was the first *Tintin In
. . .* adventure since *Tintin In The East*, the abortive title
which linked *Cigars Of The Pharaoh* and *The Blue Lotus*,
Chang's previous appearance, back in 1932. This was
originally ascribed to market research, indicating that
more people would be likely to buy a book with Tintin's
name in the title. In reality, the title reflected the solo
nature of the undertaking. Certainly, it was a more glamorous title than the three prototypes rejected in its favour:
The Cow's Snout, *The Yak's Snout* and *The Bear's Snout*.

Aside from the general whiteness at the book's heart,
there are several other clues to Hergé's state of mind
within the story. On page 40, for example, Haddock
hangs by a rope over a cliff face, the other end cutting
into Tintin's waist. If they stay there, they are both done
for. If Haddock cuts the rope, then Tintin will live.
'You at least can save yourself. You must cut the rope:
it's the only answer! . . . Better for one to die, rather
than two, isn't it?' shouts Haddock. The message for

Germaine – that the two of them were locked into something irrecoverable – was implicit.

The strong theme of telepathy and ESP that runs through the story is also tied to developments in Hergé's private life – but not directly. This was Fanny Vlaminck's hobby showing through. Like Hergé, Eastern mysticism interested her, just as it didn't interest Germaine. After a long period of isolation and separation, Hergé emerged refreshed from *Tintin In Tibet*, his guilt and white nightmares banished, determined to settle his emotional dilemma at last. He divorced Germaine and married Fanny. He had not fallen in love with Tintin again – far from it, he detested his creation for what he had been put through – but he was beginning to learn how to ignore him.

What's more, *Tintin In Tibet* did not have to scramble to a conclusion. It was slightly over-length – a page-long scene had to be cut to fit the book version, between lines 3 and 4 of page 37, in which Haddock's blazing overturned stove sets off a box of flares. That slotted out neatly, though, and for the most part the book is beautifully paced. *Tintin In Tibet* achieved its aims admirably, both artistically and emotionally. The effects of this enormous weight lifted from Hergé's shoulders can be seen in his next book, *The Castafiore Emerald*, a masterpiece of relaxation.

There were, however, other problems on the horizon. Hergé had set up his studios with the idea of emulating Disney's artistic achievements. Raymond Leblanc had an eye on Disney's commercial achievements as well.

24

'Her-jjay's Advenn-tures Of
Tinn-tinn!'

'Her-jjay's 'Advenn-tures Of Tinn-tinn!' The announcer's lurid tones prefaced every five-minute television cartoon, and froze in the minds of millions as the popular image of Tintin. Little else was memorable about Tintin on television, apart from an obsessive money-saving repetitiveness, so that each five-minute slice consisted of the second half of the previous week's episode, joined to the first half of the following week's instalment. Starting in 1959, while Hergé was in the middle of *Tintin In Tibet*, eight adventures were exploited in this way ('exploited' being the right word): the moon books, *The Crab With The Golden Claws*, the *Rackham* books, *The Shooting Star*, *The Black Island* and *The Calculus Affair*.

As to whether or not Hergé liked these cartoon versions of his stories, Bob de Moor is fairly unequivocal. 'No no no no no no no no no no no,' he remembers, notching up eleven 'no's in the process. The films were the work of Belvision, and the man behind Belvision was Raymond Leblanc. Hergé was allowed limited artistic control over his creation. Leblanc was the man with the real Disney vision, although the money was not available to do Hergé's meticulous illustrations any sort of animated justice. Michael Turner: 'There was a great attempt by Raymond Leblanc to turn the Hergé Studios into a kind of Disney with the films, first of all the partial animation and then the full animation by Belvision, run by Leblanc. Hergé didn't like them at all. Leblanc was not an evil genius, that would be putting it wrongly, but he was the guy with the exploitive eye, and Editions du Lombard (his publishing company) almost lived on Tintin in the 1960s.'

The partial animations that Turner refers to, versions of *King Ottokar's Sceptre* and *The Broken Ear* made in 1956, have not been seen for many years, like Hergé's own 1947 puppet version of *The Crab With The Golden Claws*. The fully animated Belvision cartoons are still shown around the world, however, shabbily contrasting with the book versions. Bereft of all the wit, dramatic tension and artistic skill of the originals, the films suffer from that particular cartoon affliction whereby the characters run past the same tree time and time again. (The deliberate Americanisation of the stories didn't help much either.) Students of the animated cartoon will not be surprised to learn that representatives of Messrs Hanna and Barbera came over to supervise the work in progress.

Of course, it is not surprising that some of Hergé's more complex plots were slimmed down. What is inexplicable, and irreparably damaging, is that almost all Hergé's jokes were replaced with 'witticisms' so laboured as to defy belief. Take *The Secret Of The*

Unicorn, for instance. The skilfully built-up whodunnit concerning the thefts of the model ships is replaced by two unexplained silhouettes in raincoats who mutter 'hur hur hur' to each other before walking into Tintin's house and bashing him over the head. The connected subplot of the Thompsons' search for the wallet thief is condensed into a TV appearance where they explain directly to the viewer: 'We have a plan. But our plan is a secret.' 'Oh I see,' says the interviewer. 'You're secret police.' That this is meant to be funny is only made clear immediately afterwards, when the interviewer throws in a 'ha ha ha' to point up the joke.

Hergé's reaction to the humiliation of seeing his work mutilated in public was to keep well away. Bob de Moor found himself despatched to do a supervisory job at the Belvision studios. On later cinema cartoons, Hergé himself did some of the supervisory work, providing model sheets for the animators and talking through the rushes with them; but neither he nor de Moor could elevate artistic standards on what were essentially low-budget projects. Script matters, of course, were even further out of their grasp.

Immediately after *Tintin In Tibet*, Hergé's time was taken up with another project which promised to redeem the situation, although in the end it fared little better; the live action cinema version of Tintin. Two films were made under licence by the French Pathé Company, *The Mystery Of The Golden Fleece* in 1961 and *Tintin And The Blue Oranges* in 1964. A complete unknown with no acting experience was chosen to star as Tintin. Jean-Pierre Talbot was actually a Belgian sports instructor spotted on a beach by Jacques Van Melkebeke's daughter. His physical resemblance to Tintin helped, but what clinched it was that he was consoling a tearful child at the time, just as Tintin would have done.

Unfortunately the scripts, written by three gentlemen named André Barret, Jean-Jacques Vierne and Philippe Condroyer, were little better than their animated equivalents. Aside from his friendship with Talbot, Hergé gained nothing from watching others assume they could do better than he. 'He was not very enthusiastic about *The Golden Fleece* and *The Blue Oranges*,' says Bob de Moor. 'It was very difficult for him. When you take characters out of their context it's always the same.'

The problem was really summed up by one little girl who wrote to Hergé and complained that the screen version of Haddock spoke in a different voice to the one in her books. The live action films did not continue. Jean-Pierre Talbot went off to the army to do his national service, where he emulated the problems suffered by Hergé's brother. Particularly embarrassing was the escort duty for the state visit of Queen Elizabeth and Prince Philip, when a gaggle of children wheeled out to look enthusiastic suddenly found a genuine object for their enthusiasm, discovering Tintin standing nearby in a soldier's uniform.

Belvision, meanwhile, was not finished with its activities. In 1969 Leblanc decided to move Tintin cartoons into the cinema, with an adaptation of *The Seven Crystal Balls/Prisoners Of The Sun* story. 'Greg', the editor-in-chief of *Tintin* magazine (also a highly successful illustrator in his own right), was given the task of writing the big screen version. The result was remarkable; not only did it recapture the lack of wit and ingenuity of the TV films, but it was the first Tintin story to perpetrate the heresy of abandoning Tintin's famous plus fours in favour of a pair of tight jeans. Worse was to follow with the appearance in 1972 of *Tintin And The Lake Of Sharks*. This time 'Greg' was arrogant enough to believe he could write his own Tintin story. The book version was published in the style of the other Tintin stories, a piece of near–deception alleviated by removing Hergé's name from the cover. Bob de Moor, once again, had to spend five or six years working on the background illustration, a job he was glad to finish. The completed film, needless to say, did not impress Hergé.

Professor Calculus is building a machine that will make perfect replicas of anything. He is doing it in a lonely villa by a lake in the Syldavian countryside (no explanation why). Rastapopoulos wishes to steal the machine. Instead of walking into the undefended villa and taking it, he builds a Blofeld–style giant under–water hideout under the lake (no explanation why, or how). Tintin and Haddock are flying to Syldavia. The pilot abandons the plane, to try and kill them (no explanation why, who he is, or what happened to the other passengers – but he does have shifty eyes). There is no attempt at satire, wit, observation or character comedy, but two insufferable snub–nosed kids are introduced, who apparently have no home to go to, presumably in an attempt to entice the American consumer.

It is surely a measure of how powerless Hergé was on

Tintin magazine, a publication named after the character he had created, that Greg was in a position to turn his principles upside down on Leblanc's behalf. Leblanc later observed: 'The intransigence of Hergé, who judged Greg's approach to be incompatible with his own conceptions, was certainly decisive in his disengagement . . . Hergé ceased to battle and little by little detached himself from the magazine.'[1]

There appears to have been friction between Hergé and Greg, from the appearance of the first Belvision cartoons onwards. After Hergé had so personalised Tintin with *Tintin In Tibet*, it was decided in 1960 that Greg should write the next Tintin story instead. Hergé would merely illustrate Greg's ideas. Greg wanted to return to the heights of *The Calculus Affair* with another cold war thriller entitled *Tintin In Berlin*. Hergé dutifully began work on Greg's script, but after seven pages, he refused to go any further. His rebellion took the form of a story that was the antithesis of the Greg style. Hergé made sure that in Tintin's next adventure, there would be no fights, no chases, no villains. He would create a gripping story in which absolutely nothing happened at all.

25

The Castafiore Emerald

Les Bijoux De La Castafiore

Technically, at least, *The Castafiore Emerald* is Hergé's masterpiece, marking the high tide of his creative abilities. To most critics it is the finest Tintin adventure, if not the finest comic book ever written. Others say that for all its expertise it lacks warmth and emotion. That may be so, but in its way the story says more about its author's emotional state than any other Tintin book except *Tintin In Tibet*. It is certainly Hergé's most adult adventure, a relative failure with the public in as far as it puzzled many of his younger readers. Tintin had come so far from the knockabout children's character of the Congo as to be almost unrecognisable.

The subject of the story, in as far as there is one, concerns an unexpected visit to Marlinspike by Bianca Castafiore, her maid Irma and her pianist Wagner, and the disappearance every hour or so of her jewels. Behind this light superstructure, Hergé plays a series of games with his readers – he admits as much by depicting Tintin looking directly out of the front cover illustration, finger to his lips. Structurally, the book is a catalogue of false expectations for the reader. Almost every page ends in a cliffhanger, and the atmosphere of tension never flags, without any definite result. 'My ambition was to try and tell a tale in which absolutely nothing happened, simply to see whether I was capable of keeping the reader's attention to the end,' Hergé explained. The result was wildly successful, 'a triumph of repose', as he put it.

The story is also a revealing insight into Hergé's domestic ambitions, 'a voyage around my bedroom', in his words. He had come through the trauma of parting with Germaine, of psychosomatic illness, of opening up his feelings to the world in *Tintin In Tibet*, and of 'Greg' putting a large wellington boot through some of his most cherished ideals. What he desired now, above all else, was rest and relaxation. He wanted to stay at home with Fanny, enjoying his wealth, eating, drinking and dressing well to reward himself, and avoiding the outside world wherever possible. This need shines out of every page. Remarkably, the action never once leaves the confines of the Marlinspike estate.

The character of Haddock and the character of Hergé had now become one and the same. Hergé freely admitted that he was projecting his own desire for peace and quiet on to the Captain, and offloading his frustrations in the same direction. The Captain has now come to dominate proceedings. It is the Captain who suffers on Hergé's behalf – forced to share the company of a talking parrot, virtually married off to Castafiore by *Paris Flash* magazine, drunk out of house and home by an unwanted brass band, and continually at the mercy of the incompetent builder Mr Bolt and his failure to mend a dangerous cracked step.

The parrot excepted, these were all real tribulations from Hergé's own home life. Christopher Willoughby-Drupe and Marco Rizotto of *Paris Flash* were based on a pair of genuine journalists who hung about making up lurid feature stories, an interesting modern-day contrast to Tintin's 1920s incarnation as crusading reporter. The passing brass band turned up at Hergé's house one day to perform in his honour, completely uninvited. After a quick tune, they cleaned out every bottle of alcohol in the place, then shouted out three cheers for Spirou, a comic character drawn by somebody else.

Mr Bolt the builder (M. Boullu in French) was a real-life builder, actually called Boullu. Hergé was so incensed by his unreliability that he didn't even bother to change the man's name – although needless to say, like Haddock, he continued to employ him, offering only a limp 'it was nice of you to come' when the errant workman finally showed up. Even in the relatively plush surroundings of commercial success, the values of suburban Brussels had not deserted Hergé. It took Boullu two years to complete a minor job at the Remi household, but his reputation obviously spread far and wide. When *The Castafiore Emerald* was published, Hergé was contacted by a local woman hoping to discover M. Boullu's address; he had built a terrace for her which had collapsed as he drove away.

Despite the frequent lapses in security, as the likes of Wagg and Castafiore breached his defences apparently at will, Hergé had none the less managed to find a degree of repose that had previously eluded him. The Tintin stories no longer interested him as a vehicle for straightforward adventure, or even for political satire. They were only of any use in as far as they might aid his relaxation; not just as an outlet for frustration, but also as a format to be experimented with, a set of characters and expectations to be subverted. From this point on no Tintin story proceeded conventionally in character terms. Hergé took pleasure in overturning the natural laws of his own fictional world.

In *The Castafiore Emerald*, everything is topsy-turvy. Obvious villains turn out to be harmless, crimes turn out not to have been committed, even the apparently invincible Wagg finally meets defeat, crushed by Castafiore on page 42 ('Good morning, Mr Sag'). The budding relationship between Calculus and Castafiore defies all expectations, as Cuthbert develops a considerable, even romantic attachment to the Milanese Nightingale. When this manifests itself in a new variety of rose, created by the Professor in her honour, it seems entirely reasonable that the plucked flower should conceal a renegade bee, which stings Captain Haddock viciously on the nose.

Elsewhere, Calculus' chief invention of the book, a prototype version of colour television developed some five years before the appearance of the real thing, manifestly does not work. In a brilliant sequence on pages 48–50, the conqueror of space is reduced to complete absurdity, as 'Super-Calcacolour' virtually destroys the sight of the Marlinspike guests. Curiously, in the sequence earlier in the book where a real TV crew visits Marlinspike, Hergé's always meticulous research let him down by its accuracy. The technique he depicted, using linked film and TV cameras, underwent a brief heyday *circa* 1962 before dying out. The cumbersome apparatus dates the story in a way that Tintin's celebrated trousers never could.

Such minor quibbles apart, one gets the feeling that Hergé was justifiably proud of *The Castafiore Emerald*. Little in-jokes and references abound. Three model unicorns sit in the background as the TV crew go about their work; Castafiore's emerald is a present from the Maharajah of Gopal; Snowy suddenly finds the power of speech again, to remark 'I can't stand animals who talk'; and so on and so forth. Hergé had only one criticism of the book – he felt that he had rather allowed the gypsies who start the story off to fade away, their role simplified into another red herring in the jewel hunt. Fans of *The Castafiore Emerald* tend to disagree. It is a story that inspires extraordinary loyalty in its admirers, such as the fan who wrote a book analysing it frame by frame.

When the story reached its close, Hergé had been drawing the adventures of Tintin continuously for thirty-four years. *The Castafiore Emerald* was a little rebellion of sorts, not the audience-grabbing thriller that the editorship of *Tintin* magazine had wanted. They hoped that Hergé would quickly return to the fold. Unfortunately for them, Hergé's next rebellion was slightly bigger. With the redrawing of *The Black Island* in the offing, he seized the chance to announce that there would not be another Tintin story – for the time being. After thirty-four years of solid work he refused to draw two books at once, as he had done in the past.

This time, he was to make them wait for another four years.

Eventually, it was not Casterman or Raymond Leblanc, but his curious love-hate relationship with his creation that forced Hergé back to work. As he admitted to journalist John Whitley, 'I got fed up with Tintin and tried to paint for four years . . . but if one wants to paint, it must come from here [the heart], and for me that is already occupied by Tintin, however unfortunately. So, I was caught again.'[1]

26

Flight 714

Vol 714 Pour Sydney

If Hergé had cut down dramatically on his work rate following *The Castafiore Emerald*, he certainly did not compromise on quality. Although it disappointed some critics looking for another masterpiece of structure, *Flight 714* (or *Flight 714 To Sydney*, as it is known in French, having almost become *Tintin In Indonesia*) finds him at the top of his form. Artistically, the book is his greatest achievement, especially the later scenes inside the temple and in the volcanic crater before it erupts, where the addition of airbrushing to his repertoire enriches an already lush but subtle range of water colours, gouache and pastel shades. The artwork was another collective effort by the studio, but Hergé deserves special credit for the cinematic ingenuity of his composition. With more use of the long shot and the close-up than before, almost every frame within each scene offers an intriguing variant on its predecessor.

Ostensibly, the story returns Tintin to the thriller fray. After bumping into Piotr Skut at Djakarta airport en route for Sydney, he, Haddock and Calculus hitch a lift on the private plane Skut is flying – the Carreidas

160 executive jet, property of Laszlo Carreidas, 'the millionaire who never laughs'. Out over the Indian Ocean, the jet is hijacked and flown to a small island, controlled by Sondonesian nationalist guerrillas but also home to Roberto Rastapopoulos. The editors of *Tintin* magazine heaved a sigh of relief to see their hero back in action, but Hergé did not regard *Flight 714* as conventional action at all. He had one or two surprises up his sleeve.

First, he used the book to destroy his long-standing villains, Rastapopoulos and Allan. Not that they were killed off – the ending is left purposely ambiguous – but it was certainly their farewell appearance. He dispatched them just as terminally by making them look extremely silly. Allan loses all his teeth in a tiff with a bunch of terrified Sondonesians; while Rastapopoulos dresses up in a tasteless pink 'cowboy deluxe' outfit, before having his clothes shredded, his mouth closed over with sticking plaster, his eye blacked and his head crowned with a bump which stayed with him – on greetings cards and suchlike – until Hergé's death. 'Dressed like that, Rastapopoulos was so grotesque that he ceased to threaten,' said Hergé, who when he visited Rapid City in Dakota a few years afterwards bought himself a replica of the same cowboy outfit – suggesting that there was a little of him in all his characters, even if it only crept out in front of a mirror.

This subversion of his readers' expectations was extended by a blurring of his normally clear distinction between good and evil. Having revealed his initially threatening baddies to be weak and ludicrous, some of the goodies are exposed as being not so goodie after all.

Chief amongst these is Laszlo Carreidas, the marvel-lously shabby millionaire based by Hergé upon Marcel Dassault, the aeroplane tycoon who created the Mirage jet. Although undoubtedly the party wronged by Rastapopoulos, Carreidas is scarcely any nicer than his kidnapper. Selfish, wilful and a cheat at battleships, Carreidas' best scene is where he and Rastapopoulos, under the influence of Dr Krollspell's truth serum, compete for the title of Nastiest Child In Europe. The parallel between big business and crime was fairly obvious; some things hadn't changed since *Tintin In America*.

Unusually for a later Tintin book, there are a number of new protagonists (Carreidas included), all with superbly evocative faces that instantly betray their char-acters: Spalding, long, thin, the millionaire's pompous and untrustworthy secretary, described by Hergé as 'an English public school man, obviously the black sheep of his family'.[1] Dr Krollspell, of the sunglasses and the evil laugh ('he he he'), a graduate of the Nazi charm school; Mik Kanrokitoff, the mysterious scientist and telepa-thist, based directly on Jacques Bergier of the French *Planète* magazine; and Paolo Colombani and Hans Boehm, dubious stand-in pilots whose squashed-in faces are tailor-made for the nerve-racking tension of the landing on the island, as they struggle to brake the jet on a runway far too short for the task.

Kanrokitoff's arrival halfway through the book is the signal for phase two of Hergé's subversion of the medium. At this point the machinations of Rastapopoulos are dwarfed by the discovery that the island's ancient temple is a sort of Gatwick departure lounge for passing extra-terrestrials, whose statues adorn the temple walls. This was extremely fashionable subject matter for 1966, when Erich von Däniken was launching the 'Was-God-An-Astronaut?' craze. Today such theories seem rather quaint, but at the time a lot of people were convinced that UFOs had been regularly dropping in for thousands of years to see how we were doing. Hergé was sufficiently interested in this area, and in Jacques Bergier's work in particular, to explore the subject rather gingerly in *Flight 714*. It is to his credit that the story still reads believably.

The final scenes, as the lights of the astroship appear against the night sky, guided by the flattened cone of the volcano, are extremely reminiscent of the 1977 film *Close Encounters Of The Third Kind*. It is interesting that Steven Spielberg, who directed that film, should be such a keen Tintin fan. Hergé's ending is kept far more mysterious than Spielberg's, retaining ambiguity by refusing to show anything of his extraterrestrial visitors other than a few distant lights. Instead he uses the device of cutting suddenly to a morning-after television interview with a bewildered Tintin & Co., their memories of the encounter erased. Choosing the unbelieving Wagg as his viewer makes the aliens seem pretty convincing, though.

Hergé was never satisfied with this closing passage, partly because he felt he hadn't had the courage of his convictions, and partly because he had overrun the plot and had to scramble to a conclusion once again. Despite working everything out from the beginning he somehow came out with a 64-page story, and had to cut two pages by jumping straight from the Indian Ocean to the Wagg household. He felt he had let down the effort that he and others had put into the earlier parts of the book, especially as regards the meticulous design of the revolutionary Carreidas 160 jet, a fully working aircraft with technical plans drawn up by Roger Leloup.

In 1968, however, when the story ended, he was quite prepared to let the scrambled finale pass – even though this time he had refused to let *Tintin* magazine start printing the story until he had completely finished it. After two years' hard work, he was utterly sick and tired of Tintin. 'It was during *Flight 714* that he was most troubled with the rashes on his hands,' says Michael Turner, 'and there were long periods where he couldn't work at all.' It was now that Hergé confessed to Turner, 'I've fallen out of love with Tintin. I just can't bear to see him.'

Another Tintin story in the foreseeable future was out of the question. Hergé had passed his sixtieth birthday on *Flight 714* and wanted to enjoy his retirement, Tintin-free. He bought a large house. He made plans to see the world. He announced that he had given up arguments of any description. It was time to relax. Turner recounts: 'He lived quietly and extremely well. One of the delights of visiting him was the eating – I used to come back and rave about the restaurants, like "Comme Chez Soi" and "Villa Lorraine". He would take you along to a restaurant like "Comme Chez Soi", which even then was horrendously expensive, and he wouldn't be known, no, he'd be greeted with open arms. At the time he was obviously a regular visitor.' It should be recorded that for a man in his sixties, Hergé remained slim and good-looking none the less. An appetite for fish and Loire Reds kept him in trim.

For the first time, Hergé had discovered the fruits of withdrawing his labour, a practice alien to someone with his background. Whatever his contract said, he had so much money that he had no need to work – he had *Tintin* magazine's hierarchy over a barrel – and so, by simply refusing to start another story, he began at last to achieve a degree of commercial ascendancy. This time the gap between stories was even longer – seven years. The reason given was the film version of the Peruvian adventures and its sequel *The Lake Of Sharks*, an excuse which fooled nobody. 'It was a pretext,' admits Bob de Moor.

Sadly, by the time Hergé agreed to begin work on another Tintin book, he was two years off his seventieth birthday; and whether through old age or frequent periods off work, the talent that had blossomed throughout the 1950s and 1960s was starting to wither.

27

Tintin And The Picaros

Tintin Et Les Picaros

The first thing anyone noticed was the trousers. The unimaginable had happened. After close on fifty years of sterling service, the plus fours were gone; in their place, a pair of anodyne brown trousers borrowed from the film version of *Prisoners Of The Sun*. Worse still, on the cover of *Tintin And The Picaros*, these sacrilegious replacements were flared. For the majority of Tintin fans, the sky had just about fallen in. Hergé was playing nasty games with his readership. He described Tintin's sudden fondness for his new legwear as 'the worm in the apple'.[1]

There were a myriad other changes in the new story. Tintin had taken to riding a motorcycle with a CND symbol on his helmet. He practised yoga in his spare time. Nestor, faithful, reliable Nestor, listened at doors and was caught drinking his master's whisky. General Alcazar, always so macho and self-possessed, was now under the thumb of a ghastly wife. Haddock, revealed embarrassingly as the possessor of the Christian name Archibald, described Tintin's own name as 'grotesque'.

Apparently, the only professional enjoyment left for Hergé lay in tampering substantially with his own ground rules. There was certainly some hilarity to be had in such distortions, but it concealed a long-term disaffection with his creations. 'As time went on in the late 'sixties and 'seventies, his work depressed him very much,' says Michael Turner. 'I think he felt trapped, and he did say on one occason, "I've got the responsibility of the studio, and it's not just me, I've got these dozen people who are utterly dependent on me." And it all became a bit too much.'

For *Tintin And The Picaros*, Hergé dispensed with the panoply of studio staff and retrenched. He and Bob did the book alone. Says de Moor: 'Maybe the story is good, maybe the story is bad. I don't know. Many people think it's not like the other books, other people think I drew it myself – that's not true. It was the same working method as the other books throughout. Nothing changed, except I was the only artist. Martin was gone, Roger Leloup was gone; we drew it alone, Hergé and I.'

As one would expect, *The Picaros* has many fine vignettes – Calculus absent-mindedly bathing in his dressing gown and Haddock visiting a tobacconist accompanied by a small regiment of military policemen spring to mind – but over all it is a lacklustre story, missing the sparkle of a genuine Tintin adventure. In part, Hergé had subverted expectations too far, in part his own jaded feelings showed through. Drawing Tintin running made him feel tired, he said. Both Tintin and Haddock show no desire to get up and go adventuring, or involve themselves in any way. They are happy to be led by events. They return to San Theodoros, but only because they are lured there by General Tapioca against their better instincts. When the book is over, Haddock announces, 'Blistering barnacles, I shan't be sorry to be back home in Marlinspike.' Unusually for him, Tintin adds, 'Me too, Captain . . .'

Bob de Moor explains: 'At sixty I think it was more difficult for Hergé to dream up new stories. Until the end of the war, he was a young man, he had a lot of ideas. But after sixty years he said "J'ai raconté tout". After that, to have a new idea better than the others, he had to think! He was not the sort of artist whom you asked to draw night and day until the age of 70. Sometimes he would say "I have no ideas", at other times, "yes, we're going". But it took longer and longer to think of good ideas.' Burnt out, Hergé completed only this one book in the last fifteen years of his life.

Although he strenuously denied it, the book has the air of a finale. It is stuffed full of familiar faces – Alcazar, Wagg, Dr Ridgewell from *The Broken Ear*, Colonel Sponsz, Bianca Castafiore, Irma, Wagner, Pablo (now unaccountably treacherous), Marco Rizotto and Christopher Willoughby-Drupe. Even General Tapioca shows himself for the first time, in two rather enjoyable cameos – Haddock's shouting match with his television set, which is broadcasting the General's antagonistic speech, and a conversation between Tapioca and Alcazar, lamenting the modern decline in standards which prevents them being allowed to shoot one another. It is almost as though Hergé was trying to squeeze everybody in for one last farewell performance. In the carnival sequences at the end, he even includes a number of other famous cartoon characters, prancing down a street named after his own birthday, 22 May 1907.

If *Tintin And The Picaros* does not seem as fresh as its predecessors, it is at least no less painstakingly researched and historically accurate. It is based on the Régis Debray affair, when a French writer was imprisoned in Bolivia after being falsely accused of helping the guerrilla leader Che Guevara. The city of Tapiocapolis, the renamed Los Dopicos,[2] is drawn from the Brazilian capital of Brasilia. Every leaf in the jungle is taken from a South American reference work. The Picaros themselves are based upon the Tupamaros, an Indian tribe which assisted Castro to power in Cuba. Hergé had intended to call them the Bigotudos, which means moustaches, but changed his plans to avoid confusion with the Taschist regime in Borduria. Even the secondary elements are based on truth: The Jolly Follies, Jolyon Wagg's terrible travelling concert party, is a synthesis of three real Belgian touring groups, each one crammed to the brim with real Waggs. Hergé even redrew his opening sequence at the last minute because the season portrayed was not quite right to coincide with a South American carnival.

With such a heavily researched current affairs background, *Tintin And The Picaros* cannot help being Hergé's most overtly political book for many years, but unlike his other political works there is no campaigning element. The conclusion is especially cynical. Tintin helps Alcazar to power, not for the sake of justice but merely to save his friends. The revolution achieves nothing, other than to change the uniforms of the guards patrolling the slums.

To some extent, this disillusionment reflected Hergé's own experiences in the early 1970s. For all his protestations about the time taken up by animated projects, he had spent much of the time since *Flight 714* travelling the world. He had visited Italy, England,[3] Sweden, Switzerland, Greece, Denmark, the Bahamas and Taiwan, this last being an acceptance of Madame Chiang Kai-Shek's invitation issued following publication of *The Blue Lotus*. He had also made two visits to the USA, to the Mayo Clinic in Rochester, Minnesota, in an attempt to cure the eczema that accompanied his every attempt to draw Tintin. While in America he had gone to Pine Ridge to visit the Sioux tribe on their reservation, armed with an introduction from Père Gall, the Red Indian-fixated monk. Like the Taiwanese visit, which had been conducted partly as an exercise in finding Chang, this was a nostalgic trip; the reality of old friendships did not interest him, but the symbolic innocence of his idealised past drew him like a magnet. All he found, however, was squalor and degradation. The Red Indians were dissolute, sad and drunken. Their simple nobility and heroism, which he had tried to emulate as a youth, did not exist.

Allied to this bitter disappointment were the frustrations that accompanied the discovery of Chang. The tremendous excitement of finding his old friend in 1975 was dampened by the hard reality of trying to communicate with Shanghai. The long-awaited and idealised reunion was scuppered by Chinese red tape. For the benefit of customs officers, Hergé and Chang's letters to each other had to be circumspect, couched in terms of gushing praise for Chairman Mao; discussing subjects such as art, Taoism and Eastern philosophy would have been dangerous for a Chinese from a Catholic background. Getting Tintin books into China was difficult; getting Chang out of the country, or Hergé in, seemed impossible.

The emotional reunion had to wait a further six years, until 1981. It was a major event, with TV and press present. Chang brought with him his son, whom Hergé took on at his studios, and both were given permission to stay in Europe. Despite the razzamatazz, however, one senses that the longed-for reunion did not entirely live up to expectations. For a relationship based on one year's friendship half a century before, theirs had a lot to live up to. It is revealing that Chang chose ultimately to move to Paris, rather than stay in Brussels. Perhaps the weight of expectation was too much for the pair of them. Michael Turner: 'For Hergé, the relationship with Chang had become a mystical relationship. I don't know to what extent the meeting again was a disillusionment.'

Hergé's nostalgic fantasies were crumbling before his eyes, and he was becoming more cynical. In the early 1970s he had been decorated by the Belgian government, as an Officer of the Order of the Crown. Given the events of 1944, and all his subsequent trouble with the authorities, this may not have helped. The direct consequence of this escalating cynicism was that his home life with Fanny, in contrast to his home life with Germaine, did not now involve Tintin at all. The boy reporter was barred from the Remi household. Hergé had been proud to call Germaine 'Hergée'. Now, when he got home, he preferred to think of himself as Georges Remi.

Particularly illuminating was his decision in 1971, and the second thoughts that accompanied it, to grant an extended interview to the journalist Numa Sadoul. It was the only large-scale interview he ever gave – most of the quotes attributed to Hergé in this book are taken from it – and the published results ran to 141 pages. More revealing than the interview itself, however, is what was left out. After Sadoul had finished his transcripts, Hergé vetted them as part of the deal. He spent two years reworking his answers into their definitive shape, and surprised his interviewer by cutting out reams of material which he retrospectively considered indiscreet.

Gone were all references to his early links with the political right. Gone too were his thoughts on Catholicism, on sex and on love. Revealingly, he changed the title from *Conversations With Georges Remi* to *Conversations With Hergé*. Little is known of what he originally said, but one surviving example would seem to be typical: asked whether he is travelling the world in order to flee Tintin, 'Hergé' replies, 'There's no question of fleeing, it's more a question of seeing and discovering new things, and recharging my batteries.' Originally, 'Georges Remi' had replied, 'That's partly it

– a need to play truant for a while, to escape from this hard labour, which feels like slavery.'

The only exception to this avoidance of Tintin, it seems, came when Hergé and de Moor were joking at the expense of the characters in *Tintin And The Picaros*. 'It was very curious,' recalls de Moor. 'We were laughing all the time. One day we were laughing about Alcazar when he was a little boy living with his parents in San Theodoros, and after that we thought "ah yes, and then he gets married". "Ah, but that's a good idea", said Hergé.' Peggy Alcazar was the one character who managed to intrude into the Tintin-free zone of the Remi household: Hergé saw the woman he was searching for in a television documentary, and he drew her there and then. Alcazar's dreadful wife was actually the secretary to a spokesman for the Ku-Klux-Klan.

If Hergé could subvert his characters' attitudes and behaviour as a remedy for his own boredom with Tintin, he could hardly subvert his artistic standards. The sheer perfection of the illustration process that he had instituted for each and every Tintin book mitigated against his taking pleasure from his work. For this reason, perhaps, there is something indefinable absent from Hergé's artwork in *Tintin And The Picaros* – enjoyment, perhaps. While the drawings are technically unassailable, life has not been breathed into the characters as normal. The colours are lively but indiscriminate. The illustrations are set too firmly in their time, giving the book a distinctive 1970s look. It is dated in a way that Hergé had always previously managed to avoid. Apart from an unwillingness to extend himself, advancing age was telling on Hergé in other ways. When he had finished the book he was taken aback to discover that it was 63 pages long – he had miscounted. A page had to be taken out, between pages 22 and 23, in which Colonel Sponsz repeated Rastapopoulos' routine with the spider from *Flight 714:* 'This time, I shall break them! I shall break them . . . like I break this glass!' Sponsz hurls the glass at the floor, from where it promptly rebounds into a bust of Marshal Kûrvi-Tasch, shattering the celebrated moustache.

In fact, Hergé was almost 70 when *Tintin And The Picaros* was published. There were many years of life left in him, but although nobody guessed it at the time, he had completed his last Tintin story. The will to go on had simply evaporated.

Tintin And Alph–Art

Tintin Et L'Alph'Art

Many critics like to think that the almost untranslatable *Tintin Et L'Alph'Art*[1] was set to be Hergé's last great masterpiece – but that is surely just wishful thinking. All there is to show for seven years' work are 42 pages of the roughest pencil sketches – a long, long way from a finished book. For the first time since the early 1930s, Hergé had started the story Enid Blytonstyle, with no idea of how it would end – a bad sign.[2] The plot had more than one level, but Hergé introduced them without knowing how they would eventually connect. It is difficult not to reach the conclusion that the book never stood any chance of being finished.

'I was afraid of that,' admits Bob de Moor. '*Tintin And The Picaros* took a long time, and that's not good. When we began another story I thought yes, OK, but how much time is it going to take? Maybe seven years? Ten years? I was a little afraid. I was eighteen years younger than Hergé, I had more drive. Hergé said when he was finishing *Tintin And The Picaros*, "maybe I'll do a new story when I find a very, very good idea – but it has to amuse me, I'll not do it for money or for the publishers".' Clearly, there was no hurry to get started.

The first idea Hergé had, in 1976, was to set an entire book within the confines of the departure lounge at an international airport. An airport contained 'the whole world on a reduced scale . . . tragedies, jokes, exoticism and adventure', he said. Yet all he did with this idea was talk about it. After drifting on with it for a few years, in August 1978 he changed his mind. If he could not bring himself to be interested in Tintin, why not make Tintin interested in him? Or at least, in one of his hobbies.

By 1978 Hergé's main hobby was the collection of modern art, something he could afford to indulge in expensively. Although he had flirted briefly with Expressionism, most of his acquisitions reflected a clarity of purpose similar to his own style. Warhol, Lichtenstein, Noland, Fontana, Léger, Hockney, Giacometti and a number of oriental works all decorated his clean, bare house. (The exception would seem to be an understandable fondness for Ronald Searle.) The overall effect, if you took away Hergé's greyhound, was not unlike an art gallery. 'It was very impressive to see work of that quality and currency,' says Michael Turner. 'He was obviously collecting at the top of the fashionable market.'

Something of a mutual admiration society was involved here. Andy Warhol and Roy Lichtenstein in turn were great Tintin fans. Warhol, who admired Tintin's 'great political and satirical dimensions', painted a number of portraits of Hergé. In turn, Hergé had tried his hand at a little abstract art, but was quick to abandon it. 'You paint like an illustrator,' said a perceptive friend from the Carrefour Gallery, where he often used to drop in. Despite this failure, which he happily acknow-ledged, Hergé would still sometimes slip a work of art into a Tintin story on the quiet. He included an Alfred Sisley canvas on page 10 of *The Red Sea Sharks* and a Marcel Arnould sculpture on page 11 of *Tintin And The Picaros*.

The plot of *Alph-Art*, at least as far as it went, was based on the trial of Fernand Legros, an art dealer charged with forgery. Further news stories led Hergé to add a second element, a fake religious sect. All the main characters are present – Wagg pompously scoffing at all modern art, Castafiore gullible at the other extreme and ready to be taken in by any passing charlatan. The Emir Ben Kalish Ezab gets a mention, as do W. R. Gibbons from *The Blue Lotus* and R. W. Trickler from *The Broken Ear*. Also on hand is an interesting choice of character for Hergé to revive – Ivan Ivanovitch Sakharine from *The Secret Of The Unicorn*. Even the bogus mystic Endaddine Akass has a voice that Tintin recognises at once but cannot place; perhaps because Akass looks strangely like Haddock. Like *Picaros, Alph-Art* is a nostalgic, or regressive book, depending on your point of view. The apparent re-emergence of Tintin as boy reporter would seem to confirm this.

The alphabet art element shows Hergé did have a sense of humour about his hobby. Haddock is presented with a gigantic 'H' which he is supposed to accept as a gift of deep significance and artistic perception.

Unfortunately the perpetrators of this bogus piece are linked with a conspiracy to forge copies of the real thing, which Tintin begins to unravel. For a while, Hergé decided to resurrect Rastapopoulos at the heart of this conspiracy, but dropped that idea in 1980 when he developed the alphabet element. Instead it is a previously unknown set of villains who capture Tintin at gunpoint on the Italian Isle of Ischia, and who are about to encase him in liquid polyester as a work of modern art, when the book runs out.[3]

In 1980, though, Hergé was presented with some bad news by his doctors. He was suffering from a severe form of anaemia. Officially, he was exhausted by Tintin's fiftieth anniversary celebrations the previous year, which had involved an exhibition of genuine museum artefacts used in Tintin books, a commemorative stamp issued by the Belgian post office, and a special book which Hergé sarcastically entitled *Fifty Years Of Very Happy Work*. He had drawn himself on the cover in convict's uniform, attached to a ball and chain, a huge pile of work beside him, while Tintin and the rest stood around with a whip, forcing him to draw. Other more severe drawings, such as the one where Tintin stood over Hergé with a noose ready to hang him, were kept out of sight.

Now at last Hergé had legitimate grounds to avoid going in to work, although the strain of responsibility for the studios and the guilt at not being there to supervise work still told on him. 'There was a lot of rather poor publicity work that was put out by the studio, done by the assistants,' explains Michael Turner. 'Hergé was slightly ashamed of it, I think.' It was an enfeebled Hergé that finally met Chang in 1981.

Hergé kept his sense of humour throughout. He was forced to undergo increasingly frequent blood trans–fusions, his Italian donor identified by name on the blood supplies as one Giuseppe Martini. Hergé took to blaming Martini ostentatiously for his difficulties in parking the car. Smiling courageously through a series of ups and downs, his condition deteriorated gradually until, on 25 February 1983, he suffered pulmonary failure and fell into a coma. He was rushed to the St Luc University Clinic in Brussels, where he died at 10 p.m. on 3 March. He was 75.

A wave of shock swept the French-speaking world. The death of Hergé filled the front pages *of Libération, Le Matin De Paris, Le Vif, VSD* and *L'Actualité. Le Monde* included a drawing of Tintin in Arab robes in a photo-graph of oil cartel negotiations. *Libération* went further, replacing every news photo in that issue with a relevant illustration from a Tintin book. They were humorous gimmicks desperately attempting to alleviate a simply stunning blow. An institution – the father of the European comic strip – had died.

The immediate debate concerned Tintin, abandoned on the Isle of Ischia. Should he be rescued, or left to his fate? Bob de Moor, who had worked with Hergé in his occasional dips into the story, was in no doubt. 'Personally, I would have loved to finish *Alph-Art*. It would have been a tribute to Hergé. Fanny Remi asked me to finish it, and I began to work on it, but after a few months she changed her mind. I didn't insist, but for me it was logical that there was a studio, there were artists in the studio, Casterman asked for it to be finished, there were twenty-three finished books, that one story was not finished; so I had to finish it.'

'Bob thought that he could carry on after Hergé's death,' confirms Michael Turner, 'and was very upset when family decided that should not happen, that *Alph-Art* should be preserved in aspic.' Albert Uderzo, after all, had carried on with *Asterix* after the death of René Goscinny. Hergé, though, probably would not have approved. Although he had left no definite instructions either way, he had told Numa Sadoul ten years before, 'After me there will be no more Tintin. Tintin is my creation – my blood, my sweat, my guts.' Tintin never escaped his suitably highbrow fate.

After years of disillusionment and alienation from his creation, it is pleasing to be able to relate that Hergé had actually made friends with Tintin again in the last few months of his life. Perhaps he knew he did not have long to go – nobody is quite sure – but suddenly an enthusiasm for Tintin that he had not known for years gripped him once again. 'With *Alph-Art*, the last couple of times before he died, he was returning to Tintin,' recounts Michael Turner. 'Just before he died he started to get enthusiastic again. And he kept what he was doing very very quiet. It was almost a state secret. He wouldn't tell people what he was doing, and nobody had the faintest idea what he was at. He used to drop roguish hints.' Perhaps he had thought of an ending for the story after all.

This doesn't alter the fact that *Alph-Art* probably

stood no chance of being finished, but the reconciliation was a relief to those who had watched Hergé fall out of love with Tintin over some forty years or so. It was a happy ending, of sorts, after all.

29
Post Mortem

If Hergé were to walk into his offices on the Avenue Louise tomorrow, he'd probably be almost as surprised as the staff there. None of the faces would be familiar to him – no Bob de Moor, no Jacques Martin, no Roger Leloup, in fact no working artists at all. For the Studios Hergé has now become the Fondation Hergé, a charitable foundation that dispenses worldwide merchandising franchises, and exercises an iron creative control over what can and cannot be done in Hergé's name.

Most of the commercially available Tintin T-shirts, Tintin posters, Tintin notepads, Tintin graph paper, Tintin bedcovers and so forth reach a standard that Hergé, in so far as such things interested him, would have heartily approved of. Sadly, the same cannot be said of many of the official texts that accompany the merchandise. He would not have been impressed to read the sort of pseudo-academic nonsense being published in an attempt to cement his status as an icon. He always objected to being lionised, but the style in which he is lionised today cuts right against the rules he laid down concerning clarity, wit and simplicity. Instead of describing Hergé as a talented but infuriating artist who jeopardised their successful magazine by failing to prevent his private life intruding into his work, Editions du Lombard describe Hergé's impact thus: 'The drawing of the characters, sketched after life but none the less a caricature, exemplifies the style of which we have spoken; it allows the advent of a myth. This picks up already admitted convictions, interests already present in us. It is not content just to add to them, it organises and weaves relationships between them, opposes them and makes them pass one into another. It combines them, sometimes in a very complex manner, and that stimulates our desire to comment in turn, and therefore to take part in a magic way in two universes at once'.[1] Patent nonsense, in any language.

The death of Hergé left the studios initially rudderless. He may have been a disenchanted leader, even an absentee one at times, but he was none the less strong. There was no provision for a successor. He had not expected Tintin to continue. Of course, he understood the importance of commercial exploitation, but, as Michael Turner relates, 'he wasn't always very happy about that kind of thing'. Enormous amounts of immensely valuable old material have come to light since 1983, filed away and forgotten by Hergé, who considered it extraneous to the Tintin story he was working on at the time. It was clear, soon after his death, that there was still much of value in what he had left behind.

The workers at the coalface, the artists who were Hergé's friends and colleagues, had the skill to continue, but neither Hergé nor his wife had given them a mandate to do so. Fanny had the authority, but at this stage, insufficient inclination – or perhaps experience – to take over. The artists' future was uncertain, but few of them could have suspected that within a couple of years they would for the most part be working elsewhere, and that the studios would be under the management of a new chief, Alain Barain.

Fanny Remi had struck up a close friendship with Alain Barain during the later years of her husband's life, and frequently visited the Barain household. At roughly the same time, Hergé's longtime secretary Baudouin Van Den Branden was unwell, and Madame Van Den Branden was attempting to fill in for her husband. Fanny suggested that Alain Barain take over Branden's administrative role. Barain gained access to the figures and balance sheets, and could see for himself the huge sums passing into the company, sums which Hergé found profoundly uninteresting as long as he was able to live in comfort. It was not long before Fanny's young friend was running the company for her.

A new drive was set in train after Hergé's death, to centralise power and rights on the studios. Casterman, which had exclusive rights to the book version of any new story, inevitably found its bargaining power diminished by the fact that there wouldn't be any new stories. Bereft of new material *Tintin* magazine folded, and Raymond Leblanc's controlling interest in Tintin reverted to Hergé's estate – although he did retain a sizeable stake. Ironically, only through the death of their founder had the Studios Hergé acquired the kind of autonomy that he had always desired.

At this point, two new characters came into the frame. Jane Taylor, a South London graphic designer and lifelong Tintin fan, designed a range of impressive articles initially based around Snowy, while her business partner Nick Rodwell obtained a coveted licence to manufacture them. They opened 'Pilot', a shop in Covent Garden targeted at the adult market, obtaining the rights for so long unexploited in the UK. The experiment was wildly successful, and before long branches of the renamed 'Tintin Shop' were opening up in Barcelona, Tokyo, Kyoto, and – to the chagrin of Belgian Tintin fans – Brussels itself. The pair set up their own publishing company, Sundancer, which brought out the English-language versions of *Tintin In The Land Of The Soviets*, and *Tintin And Alph'Art*. They also took over Casterman's business in the UK, and helped to mount Tintin's sixtieth-anniversary exhibition.

It was not long before Rodwell, younger and more dynamic than Barain, had formed an equally close relationship with Fanny Remi. Soon afterwards, Barain found himself completely ousted from his position as overlord of both the Hergé Foundation and its merchandising company, along with his immediate circle. Today Fanny Remi herself takes a much stronger decision-making role. The Studios Hergé have been wound up, and all design work is subcontracted. The Foundation is in the charge of Nick Rodwell and Philippe Goddin, while Jane Taylor oversees Tintin shops and their contents worldwide. 'It's like a goldmine,' enthuses Rodwell about his new position. 'There's a phenomenal market out there, but the idea is to keep it special.'[2]

One of the Hergé Foundation's most important tasks, not unnaturally, is to police pirates who make a living from selling substandard Tintin merchandise. This role has been zealously extended to take in the guardianship of Tintin and Hergé's public image, irrespective of past realities. Yet it is not necessarily the case that Hergé's memory has need of such earnest guardianship. His actions speak perfectly clearly for themselves. If he had been concerned about his public image he would not have followed his King's wishes and returned to Brussels in 1940. Whatever agonies of doubt he went through in his personal life, he remained stubbornly confident that Tintin and Haddock, his two public personae, had always done the right thing in the circumstances. His decisions should therefore be left to stand or fall on their own merits. Indeed, if they are allowed to do so, his integrity shows through clearly.

Today there are various parties, officially allied to each other, which exercise varying degrees of control over the body of Hergé's work. First, there is the Fanny Remi–Nick Rodwell grouping, which holds the rights over the Tintin characters. Then there are the various publishers worldwide: Casterman, long-term guardian of Tintin's dignity and holders of the copyright on the books, together with all the owners of the Tintin translations across the globe. Lastly there is Leblanc's Editions du Lombard, which owns the material from *Tintin* Magazine and all the animated cartoons, as well as holding a stake in the rights. It would be an optimist indeed who might think that the corporate in-fighting between the parties that has characterised the period since Hergé's death is now finished.

In Belgium, Bob de Moor ponders whether or not Casterman will last the course. 'I wonder how long they will keep the rights to Tintin,' he says. 'It's very worrying.' A close associate of Hergé, still involved in the Tintin business, reflected: 'I would think that there's inevitably going to be a fair amount of scrapping going on and it's pretty undignified.'

Any divergence between what Hergé intended Tintin to represent, and what he might now represent in commercial terms, would indeed be regrettable. Perhaps that's a naïve thing to say; but then, Tintin managed to be naïve and get away with it.

30
Conclusion

Over a hundred million books sold. Translated into over forty languages. Pressed to reveal the secret of Tintin's phenomenal success, Hergé said, 'I don't know. I absolutely don't know. I'm amazed with his success. I receive letters from all parts of the world, and I'm always surprised that an Indian boy, or even a Chinese boy, writes to me and says that he loves Tintin.'[1] His colleagues and admirers put it down to indefinable genius. His first wife put it down to hard work. The answer probably lies somewhere between the two.

The word 'genius' is easily bandied about. Hergé was an illustrator of enormous talent, influence and significance. He could be described as the father of the European *Bande Dessinée* tradition of comic illustration, a movement little known or understood in the UK where the cartoonist is king. The influence of the 'clear line' style pioneered by Hergé can be gauged by a quick look around any bookshop in France or Belgium. Scores of volumes can be seen in the Hergé style, attempting to follow the same artistic and commercial path. Yet Hergé's drawing skills were not instinctive, they were painstakingly cultivated. Although highly competent, he sometimes laboured in other mediums. Can a non-instinctive talent be described as genius? Perhaps not. His innovative experimentation with composition and structure mark him out as an artist of exceptional self-taught ability, but maybe not as an artist of genius.

Much the same can be said of Hergé the storyteller. He was a great storyteller, who knew how to hold the attention; but he was not a natural. Again, he created his own set of rules for others to follow, painstakingly revising the structure of each book, until the last frame of every page acted as a teaser for its successor. He developed techniques for the slow introduction of suspense and the sudden injection of surprise. Some of his finest achievements, though, like *The Calculus Affair* or *Flight 714*, were let down in the final analysis by their dramatic structure.

What, then, of Hergé the social commentator? The Tintin books map out the twentieth century. Initially, they stayed abreast of new technology, such as television; after the war they began to anticipate developments in the field of space travel and aircraft design. In the political arena, they trace Europe's awakening from colonialism, and the rise of the right in the 1930s, through to the cold war and beyond. At times, they managed to ripple the waters of international politics.

The secret of Tintin's success, though, is that each story, whatever its significance at the time of writing, transcends the boundaries of its setting today. Each year, more Tintin books are sold worldwide than in any other previous year, mostly to readers who accept space travel as a normal fact of life and to whom the Sino-Japanese conflict surrounding the Shanghai settlement in the 1930s means absolutely nothing. Cultural pointers to a particular time and place – Tintin's famous trousers being a case in point – pass the readers of Tintin by without impinging on their appreciation of a story. Tintin has barely dated at all, which is often the test of great literature.

To Hergé, the universality of Tintin's appeal was of far more importance than his worth as a social commentator. By turns, Tintin was innocent, politically crusading, escapist and finally cynical. Hergé's principles were constant and generally admirable throughout, but a degree of life-preserving expediency ensured that Tintin was not always able to follow suit. Hergé was a powerful social and political commentator, but events dictated that he would never mature into a commentator of genius.

Where, then, did Hergé's genius lie? Undoubtedly, in the field of humour; he was a comic genius. It was Hergé's sense of humour that made the appeal of Tintin truly international. His comedy was essentially character comedy, and his characters were universal. His jokes were mainly visual, instantly appreciable from Dacca to Droitwich, without ever being simplistic. Behind the placid surface of Hergé's personality, undisturbed by the trials and tribulations of his life, lay a rich vein of humour which charmed everyone he met. It is a strange person indeed – adult or child – who does not find funny the sight of two undercover detectives trying to board an oil freighter carrying shrimp nets.

Without Tintin, Hergé's life would have been a lot simpler, and a lot less rich. He could have avoided being variously reviled and claimed as their own by the political right and left,[2] not to mention manipulation – as he saw it – by businessmen, long periods of depression, painful soul-searching and psychosomatic illness. Yet given the chance to lead his life all over again without Tintin, Hergé would almost certainly have refused. Behind his anger and frustration at being unable to escape his protégé lay a deep, almost paternal affection for him. A few years before his death, he sent a drawing to Leslie Lonsdale-Cooper, with the revealing dedication, 'To Leslie Lonsdale-Cooper, who did so much for my little son.'[3] He and Tintin truly had a love-hate relationship.

In 1964 Hergé wrote Tintin an open letter, the most significant part of which reads as follows:

Perfect . . . if anyone is, it's you Tintin. I ought to find this quite overwhelming. Why then do I have a sense of disappointment? . . . I had set great store by Captain Haddock. Because you two spent so much time together he was bound to bring himself under control through your influence, and that part of it worked; but as for you, you absorbed none of his harsher traits, none of his frailties, you took nothing from him, not even a tot of whisky . . . My wrist was seized by an angel, colleague of that angel who now and then would rescue Snowy from the slippery slope. I had every right to launch your career, but all the same, it isn't up to a father to guide his son in the choice of his shortcomings! Salutations, my young fellow . . . I salute you.[4]

The Tintin Books

	Newspaper/ Mag Version Started	Black-and-White Book Published	Colour Book Published	English Trans-lation
Tintin In The Land Of The Soviets (Tintin Au Pays Des Soviets)	1929	1930	—	1989
Tintin In The Congo (Tintin Au Congo)	1930	1931	1946	1991
Tintin In America (Tintin En Amérique)	1931	1932	1946	1978
Cigars Of The Pharaoh (Les Cigares Du Pharaon)	1932	1934	1955	1971
The Blue Lotus (Le Lotus Bleu)	1934	1936	1946	1983
The Broken Ear (L'Oreille Cassée)	1935	1937	1943	1975

	Newspaper/ Mag Version Started	Black-and- White Book Published	Colour Book Published	English Trans- lation
The Black Island (L'Ile Noire)	1937	1938	1943 + 1966	1966
King Ottokar's Sceptre (Le Sceptre d'Ottokar)	1938	1939	1947	1958
Land Of Black Gold (Tintin Au Pays De l'Or Noir)	1939	–	1950 + 1971	1972
The Crab With The Golden Claws (Le Crabe Aux Pinces d'Or)	1940	1941	1943	1966
The Shooting Star (L'Etoile Mystérieuse)	1941	–	1942	1961
The Secret Of The Unicorn (Le Secret De La Licorne)	1942	–	1943	1952 + 1959
Red Rackham's Treasure (Le Trésor De Rackham Le Rouge)	1943	–	1944	1952 + 1959
The Seven Crystal Balls (Les Sept Boules De Cristal)	1943	–	1948	1963

	Newspaper/ Mag Version Started	Black-and-White Book Published	Colour Book Published	English Trans-lation
Prisoners Of The Sun (Le Temple Du Soleil)	1946	—	1949	1963
Destination Moon (Objectif Lune)	1950	—	1953	1959
Explorers On The Moon (On A Marché Sur La Lune)	1952	—	1954	1959
The Calculus Affair (L'Affaire Tournesol)	1954	—	1956	1960
The Red Sea Sharks (Coke En Stock)	1956	—	1958	1960
Tintin In Tibet (Tintin Au Tibet)	1958	—	1960	1962
The Castafiore Emerald (Les Bijoux De La Castafiore)	1961	—	1963	1963
Flight 714 (Vol 714 Pour ydney)	1966	—	1968	1968
Tintin And The Picaros (Tintin Et Les Picaros)	1975	—	1976	1976

	Newspaper/ Mag Version Started	Black-and- White Book Published	Colour Book Published	English Trans- lation
Tintin And Alph-Art (Unfinished) (Tintin et L'Alph'Art)	–	1986	–	1990

Acknowledgments

With thanks to Viv Drew, Michèle Kimber (they typed it), Gordon Thompson, Michael Turner, Leslie Lonsdale-Cooper, Jane Taylor, Bob de Moor, and M. Jacques Demol, Directeur de la Philatelie at the Regie des Postes, Brussels.

Notes

Chapter 1

1 *L'Actualité*, 6.3.83.
2 Quoted in *Hergé* by Thierry Smolderen and Pierre Sterckx, Casterman.

Chapter 2

1 *Sunday Times*, 1.9.68.

Chapter 3

1 Inscribed by Mussolini, 'To Norbert Wallez, friend of Italy and of Fascism, with affection and comradeship, 1924'.
2 *News Chronicle*, 6.12.58.
3 *Sunday Times*, 1.9.68.

Chapter 4

1 Page numbers are referred to as they appeared in the magazine. The numbering of the book version of *Tintin In The Land Of The Soviets* is irregular.
2 The translation of 'Milou' as 'Snowy' was a compromise, explains translator Leslie Lonsdale-Cooper, brought about in

part by the need for a five-letter name which would fit those speech bubbles where Tintin addressed his dog.

3 *Sunday Times*, 1.9.68.
4 BBC Radio Four, 24.6.77.

Chapter 5

1 *Mail On Sunday*, Associated Newspapers, 27.11.88.
2 *Time Out*, 9.8.89.

Chapter 6

1 Page 30 of the original *Petit Vingtième* story.
2 Page 53 of the *Petit Vingtième* version.
3 Page 84 of the *Petit Vingtième* version.
4 Page 90 of the *Petit Vingtième* version.
5 The meeting takes place on page 10 of the *Petit Vingtième* version.
6 Page 110 of the *Petit Vingtième* version.
7 Where it appears on page 19.

Chapter 7

1 'Je dirai même plus' in the original French.
2 Page 10 of the *Petit Vingtième* version.
3 In the original version, Mr and Mrs Snowball were introduced as being 'of the India and India bank'.
4 Page 26 of the *Petit Vingtième* version.
5 Patrash Pasha, who also gets a mention in the *Red Sea Sharks*, appears to have been a forerunner of the later Bab El Ehr.

Chapter 8

1 Page 84 of the *Petit Vingtième* version.
2 *Les Amis d'Hergé*.
3 Page 110 of the *Petit Vingtième* version.
4 Page 90 of the *Petit Vingtième* version.

5 It has been suggested that the sign of Kih-Oskh, from the *Tintin In The East* duology, was derived from the Taoist symbol of Yin and Yang. It is doubtful, however, that Hergé had ever heard of Taoism when he began the story, prior to meeting Chang.

Chapter 9

1 Hergé had read about it in the always informative *Le Crapouillot*.
2 Pages 64–73 of the *Petit Vingtième* version.
3 Pages 96–109 of the *Petit Vingtième* version.
4 On what is now page 2, between lines 3 and 4.

Chapter 10

1 Pages 54 and 107 respectively.
2 British Railways, however, refused to lend de Moor a guard's uniform 'for security reasons'. When the book appeared in England, BR wrote to Methuen to protest that Tintin's ride on the train roof set a bad example to British children, who should be encouraged to remain in their seats.
3 Page 54 of the *Petit Vingtième* version.
4 Page 10 of the *Petit Vingtième* version.
5 The trade name was dropped at Methuen's request.

Chapter 11

1 The Tintin mystery column now had a whole page of readers' plot suggestions every week in the *Petit Vingtième*, entitled 'The Tintin Inquest'.
2 *Sunday Times*, 1.9.68.

Chapter 12

1 Page 56 of the *Petil Vingtième* version.
2 Yes, they do. They climb up the steel hawsers from the dockside.

Chapter 13

1 In many cases, it was impossible to translate Hergé's original expletive into English. The replacements came mainly from Roget's *Thesaurus*, and from four other books on Leslie Lonsdale-Cooper's shelves: Petersen's *Prehistoric Life on Earth*, and *Reptiles, Mammals and Fishes of the World* by Hans Hvass (Methuen).

2 BBC Radio, 1978.

Chapter 14

1 The SS *Valmy* in the original version.

2 It was also the name of a character in *Tintin and Alph-Art*. It means 'Colorado Beetle' in French.

Chapter 15

1 Although the unfinished *Tintin And Alph-Art* hints at a nostalgic re-emergence of the reporter role.

2 Historical but not meteorological. Experts at the National Maritime Museum have since suggested that the two ships on page 18 would not have remained vertical for long at such an angle to the wind.

3 Carlsen also publishes Tintin in Sweden, see *Tintin in the Congo*.

4 In *The Crab With The Golden Claws*, the Captain blubs for his mother after a few bottles too many.

Chapter 16

1 Some critics have pointed to the early American strip *The Katzenjammer Kid* as another possible source of inspiration, with its dotty professor and bearded sailor characters; but this is unlikely, if only for the time lapse and the fact that Hergé was usually fairly open about his source material.

Chapter 17

1 It was not until he visited London in 1958 and met the Belgian ambassador that Hergé regained any sort of official approval.

Chapter 18

1 Letter to the author 31.1.90.
2 *Les Amis de Hergé*.
3 *Tintin* Magazine, Editions du Lombard.

Chapter 19

1 Quoted in *Hergé et Tintin Reporters*, Philippe Goddin, Eds. du Lombard. Trans. Michael Farr for Sundancer.
2 ibid.

Chapter 21

1 The author's thanks to Harry Marshall.
2 *Les Amis de Hergé*.
3 ibid.
4 ibid.
5 *News Chronicle*, 6.12.58.

Chapter 22

1 *Hergé et Tintin Reporters*, Editions du Lombard. Trans. Michael Farr for Sundancer.

Chapter 23

1 *Land Of Black Gold* was known in the original French as *Tintin In The Land Of Black Gold*. For no apparent reason, the English version of *The Broken Ear* calls itself *Tintin And The Broken Ear* on the spine only.

Chapter 24

1 Quoted in *Hergé et Tintin Reporters*, Philippe Goddin, Eds. du Lombard. Trans. Michael Farr for Sundancer.

Chapter 25

1 *Sunday Times*, 1.9.68.

Chapter 26

1 *Sunday Times*, 1.9.68.

Chapter 27

1 *Sunday Times*, 1.9.68.
2 Perhaps as a result of advancing old age, Hergé made a minor error, unspotted by his translators. He referred to the city as 'Los Dopicos', whereas in *The Broken Ear* it had in fact been called 'Las Dopicos.'
3 Hergé became something of an anglophile in the process. He told Olga Franklin of the *Daily Mail*, 'I like the English style of life. I feel more at home here in London than I do in Paris.'

Chapter 28

1 The 'Alph' being short for 'Alphabet'.
2 In the rough text, Hergé also got the Marlinspike telephone number wrong, an unthinkable error.
3 Because of the roughness of the sketches, there is a mistake on page 41 of the French version, where Tintin's gaoler speaks through the bars of his cell door. The dialogue, listed separately, ascribes this voice to a loudspeaker on the wall.

Chapter 29

1 *Hergé et Tintin Reporters*, by Philippe Goddin, Eds. du Lombard. Trans. Michael Farr for Sundancer.
2 *Time Out* Magazine, 9.8.89.

Chapter 30

1 BBC Radio Four, 24.6.77.
2 In 1976 Hergé told *The Brussels Bulletin*, 'For years the left has said I'm right and the right has said I'm left. I don't like to contradict either.'
3 Hergé to Leslie Lonsdale-Cooper, 25.6.77.
4 'Quelque part en France', broadcast by Inter Variétés, 21.6.64.

Bibliography

Les Amis De Hergé (June 1985, No. 1)
Les Amis De Hergé (December 1985, No. 2)
Les Amis De Hergé (June 1986, No. 3)
Archives Hergé No. 1 (Casterman, 1973)
Archives Hergé No. 3 (Casterman, 1979)
Archives Hergé No. 4 (Casterman, 1980)
Hergé 1922–1932 – Les Débuts D'un Illustrateur (Casterman, 1987)
The Making Of Tintin (Methuen, 1983)
Le Musée Imaginaire De Tintin (Casterman, 1980)
Le Temple Du Soleil (Casterman, 1988)
Tintin magazine version
Philippe Goddin, *Hergé Et Tintin Reporters* (Editions du Lombard, Bruxelles, 1986)
Benoit Peeters, *Le Monde De Hergé* (Casterman, 1983)
Numa Sadoul, *Entretiens Avec Hergé* (Casterman, 1983)
Thierry Smolderen & Pierre Sterckx, *Hergé: Portrait Biographique* (Casterman, 1988)
'Tintin cross the channel', *Times Literary Supplement* 05.12.58
'My son Tintin', *News Chronicle* 06.12.58

'Tintin', *New Statesman* 13.11.64

'Tintin in Tartan', *Times Literary Supplement* 19.05.66

'The strange case of Tintin and the cake', John Whitley, *Sunday Times* 01.09.68

'Oh, it's tough being Tintin', Olga Franklin, *Daily Mail* 05.09.68

'Tintin touches all the world', J. B. Grant, *San Francisco Review Of Books*, December 1975

'Tintin: everyone's favourite boy detective', Rona Dobson, *Brussels Bulletin* 21.05.76

'Tintin Orphelin', *L'Actualité* 06.03.83

'Ta Ta Tintin', Rayner Hardcastle, *Evening Courier* 25.08.83

'Tintin – the last chapter', *Sunday Times* 28.08.83

'Xenophobia for beginners', Valentine Cunningham, *Times Literary Supplement* 25.11.83

'Thundering typhoons! It's the Tintin bandwagon', John Coldstream, *Daily Telegraph* 15.01.88

Index

Read more . . .

Harry Thompson

PENGUINS STOPPED PLAY: Eleven Village
Cricketers Take on the World

**It seemed a simple enough idea at the outset: assemble a
team of eleven men to play cricket on each of the seven
continents of the globe**

Except – hold on a minute – that's not a simple idea *at all*. And when
you throw in incompetent airline officials, amorous Argentine
colonels' wives, cunning Bajan drug dealers, gay Australian waiters,
overzealous American anti-terrorist police, idiotic Welshmen dressed
as Santa Claus, Archbishop Desmond Tutu and whole armies of pitch-
invading Antarctic penguins, you quickly arrive at a whole lot more
than you bargained for.

Harry Thompson's hilarious book tells the story of one of those great
madcap enterprises that only an Englishman could have dreamed up, and
only a bunch of Englishmen could possibly have wished to carry out.

'As funny as you'd expect from the writer of *Have I Got News For You*'
Daily Express

'Rare, clever, creative . . . A maverick, pushing boundaries with
outrageous jokes' *Guardian*

'Crammed with sharp observation, comic and cruel characterisation
and a great many very good jokes . . . Gloriously funny and life-
affirming' *Daily Telegraph*

*Order your copy now by calling Bookpoint on 01235 827716 or
visit your local bookshop quoting ISBN 978-0-7195-6346-1*
www.johnmurray.co.uk

Read more . . .

Justin Pollard

THE INTERESTING BITS: The History You Might Have Missed

Did you give your school history lessons your undivided attention?

Even if you did, you're probably none the wiser as to how Henry II of France came to have a two-foot splinter in his head; or where terms like bunkum, maverick and taking the mickey come from; or why Robert Pate hit Queen Victoria on the head with a walking stick. Relegated to the footnotes, history's little gems are often forgotten. But *The Interesting Bits* rights this wrong; it is a veritable treasure trove of all those surprising, eccentric, chaotic, baffling asides that make history fun.

'Newsflash: history can be entertaining *and* interesting . . . an energetic, colourful book' *Easy Living*

Order your copy now by calling Bookpoint on 01235 827716 or visit your local bookshop quoting ISBN 978-1-84854-100-9
www.johnmurray.co.uk

Read more . . .

Chris Ayres

WAR REPORTING FOR COWARDS

An extraordinary true story

Chris 'risk-averse' Ayres saw journalism as his ticket to schmoozing
with celebrities and penning pompous opinion pieces. Instead he
lands a ticket to Iraq. When his boss offers to embed him with the
Marines, he's too cowardly to say no. But he (only just) lives to
regret it.

'A new genre: a rip-roaring tale of adventure and derring-don't'
Toby Young

'Brilliant . . . An unlikely, even incredible story . . . It tells the truth
about war in a way that most memoirs don't' Martin Bell

'Impressive and original' *Daily Telegraph*

'Reminded me of the granddaddy of the genre, Evelyn Waugh's
Scoop . . . Truly indispensable' *New York Times*

Read more . . .

John Betjeman, ed. Stephen Games

BETJEMAN'S ENGLAND

An affectionate and unabashed celebration of Englishness from one of the nation's most popular poets

For more than half a century, Betjeman's writings have awakened readers to the intimacy of English places — from the smell of gaslight in suburban churches, to the hissing of backwash on a shingle beach. Betjeman is England's greatest topologist: whether he's talking about a town hall or a teashop, he gets to the nub of what makes unexpected places unique.

'Betjeman chronicles the English way of life in exquisite, affectionate and often hilarious detail' *Independent*

'Remarkable . . . This is a real treat for any fan of Betjeman' *Sunday Telegraph*

Order your copy now by calling Bookpoint on 01235 827716 or visit your local bookshop quoting ISBN ISBN 978-1-84854-092-7 www.johnmurray.co.uk

Read more...

Selina Hastings

THE SECRET LIVES OF SOMERSET MAUGHAM

The definitive biography of one of the twentieth century's greatest writers

Somerset Maugham (1874–1965) was one of the most famous writers in the world, yet he lived much of his life under cover. A spy in both world wars, predominantly homosexual, though married with a child, Maugham led a dramatic double life as exciting and intriguing as any in his own brilliant novels and short stories.

'Selina Hastings's life of Maugham is pitch-perfect: supple, confident and written with something of the same beady detachment (and enjoyable signature streak of malice) as the great story-teller himself' *Daily Telegraph*

'Literary biography could hardly be better done' *The Spectator*

Order your copy now by calling Bookpoint on 01235 827716 or visit your local bookshop quoting ISBN 978-0-7195-6555-7 www.johnmurray.co.uk

From Byron, Austen and Darwin
to some of the most acclaimed and original
contemporary writing, John Murray takes pride in
bringing you powerful, prizewinning, absorbing
and provocative books that will entertain you
today and become the classics of tomorrow.

We put a lot of time and passion into what we
publish and how we publish it, and we'd like to
hear what you think.

Be part of John Murray – share your views with us at:

www.johnmurray.co.uk
▶️ johnmurraybooks
🐦 @johnmurrays
f johnmurraybooks